MONEY IS A THING

Life Tools & Cash Rules

Jay Robinson

M.I.A.T. Media Group

Copyright © 2022 Jay Robinson

All rights reserved

It is not legal to reproduce, duplicate, or transmit any part of this document in either electronic means or printed format. Recording of this publication is strictly prohibited.

No part of this book may be reproduced, or stored in a retrieval system, or transmitted in any form or by any means, electronic, mechanical, photocopying, recording, or otherwise, without express written permission of the publisher.

ISBN: 9798372186644

Cover design by: M.I.A.T. Media Group
Printed in the United States of America

This book is dedicated to:

Paula, Ellis, & Bella.

CONTENTS

Title Page
Copyright
Dedication
Introduction ... 1
PART I: Financial Fundamentals ... 2
Chapter One: Money Minded ... 3
Chapter Two: Wealth & Health ... 24
Chapter Three: Budget & Savings ... 47
Chapter Four: Credit ... 58
PART II: Assets & Liabilities ... 71
Chapter Five: Real Estate ... 72
Chapter Six: Cars ... 120
Chapter Seven: Investments ... 146
Chapter Eight: Starting Your Own Business ... 161
Chapter Nine: Starting a Nonprofit ... 171
Chapter Ten: Taxes ... 180
PART III: Bonus ... 186
Family & Friends ... 187
Life Tools & Cash Rules ... 193
Acknowledgement ... 211
About The Author ... 213

INTRODUCTION

In a culture consumed by the "Money aint a thing" mantra, I felt it was time to rewrite the narrative. In fact, if you are reading this book congratulations and thanks, as we are one step closer to changing that narrative. That said, allow me to introduce "Money Is a Thing". "Money Is a Thing" is not only a book focused on financial literacy, but it is also a collection of life tools and cash rules. See money is not simply about cars, clothes, and jewelry. Money represents freedom and the power to create change. It is a tool we can each obtain and learn to use for the creation of generational wealth. It all starts with our mindset and becoming Money Minded. So do not wait. Take action now. Begin your journey to financial freedom. Use this book to help enhance your life, your family's life, and the generations to follow.

PART I: FINANCIAL FUNDAMENTALS

In the first part of the book, we are going to go over our basic financial fundamentals. We know everyone wants to "get rich quick", but without these financial fundamentals you may find yourself running in place.

CHAPTER ONE: MONEY MINDED

Are you Money Minded? Do you know what it means to be Money Minded? If the answer to these questions is no, this will be the most important chapter of this book. Having a disciplined and positive money mindset and becoming Money Minded will help you establish a foundation for financial success. Becoming Money Minded will also help you reach your financial goals and put you on a path to financial freedom.

Put simply, being Money Minded means having a disciplined and positive mindset when it comes to money. With that said, to become Money Minded you may need to change the way you define or view money. The Webster's dictionary defines money as "something generally accepted as a medium of exchange, a measure of value, or a means of payment". The truth is money is much more than a means of payment. Money can represent wealth, freedom, power, or status. Unfortunately for some, money can also represent stress, anxiety, and fear. Remember being Money Minded means having a positive mindset. If you have a negative view towards money, it will be important to work on shifting your mindset. To do this you must first establish a positive view or definition of money. Over the years I have found that rather than focus on money, it is better to focus on wealth. There are five key elements of wealth. In this chapter we will break down the elements of wealth. Understanding each of these elements will be important in shifting your mindset and becoming Money Minded.

WEALTH MINDSET

When people think of being wealthy, they often equate it to being rich. However, a person can be rich and not wealthy. That is because being rich is simply about having a high income. The truth is, if you make $200,000 a year, but spend $250,000 a year, you might appear rich, but you certainly won't be wealthy. In fact, it doesn't matter how much money you have; if you spend more than you make, achieving wealth will be impossible. We have all seen the Instagram posts of people driving nice cars, wearing designer clothes, and taking exotic vacations. If this is your view of wealth, remember wealth is not defined by a lifestyle. Wealth is defined by a legacy. With that said, to be Money Minded you must focus on being wealthy and never on being rich. To better understand what it means to be wealthy, we must first look at what wealth is. Simply put, wealth is abundance. However, wealth is not just an abundance of money. True wealth is having abundance in all aspects of life. That means in addition to having Financial Wealth, you must also have Physical, Spiritual, Social, and Time Wealth. Some people are surprised to find out that there are several types of wealth. That's because in today's society Financial Wealth gets all the attention. Despite this, to truly have wealth and abundance you should work to amass all five types of wealth. In the end it will only help your pursuit of Financial Wealth and will also help you become Money Minded. Next we will look at the five types of wealth. Remember, acquiring each type of wealth could require years of dedication and practice. Nonetheless wealth is not defined by a lifestyle, wealth is defined by a legacy. The pursuit of wealth should be seen as a lifelong process that doesn't end, but only grows.

FINANCIAL WEALTH

The most popular and recognizable form of wealth is Financial Wealth. Generally, when people say someone is wealthy, they are referring to their Financial Wealth. Remember not to confuse Financial Wealth with being rich. That is because Financial Wealth is less about how much money you make and more about how much money you spend. With that said, the most common measure of Financial Wealth is net worth. Net worth is the value of all assets, minus the total of all liabilities. Put simply, imagine having to sell everything you own and pay back everything you owe. Whatever money is left over would be considered your net worth. With that in mind the goal of Financial Wealth is to maintain and grow a positive net worth. To do this it is important to live within your means and always invest. Don't go broke trying to look rich, or get stuck between needing to save money and the mindset of you only live once. This means you can't save what is left after spending, you must spend what is left after saving. Again, growing Financial Wealth is not about how much money you make but more about how much money you keep. If you can stay on budget, remain disciplined in your savings, and create a plan for investment, you will begin building a strong financial foundation.

Remember, money will match your mindset. If you want to become Money Minded, it is important to amass all five types of wealth. It is unfortunate but most people assume Financial Wealth will create happiness. We live in a culture of "get rich or die trying" and a mindset of "it's all about the money". On the flip side, I'm sure you have heard the sayings "money can't buy happiness" and "more money more problems". The fact is, there is some truth to all these sayings. Science has proven that money can create happiness but only up to a point. This means once a person's basic needs for food, shelter, and security are met, an increase in money will have less of an effect on happiness. For example, imagine you are hungry. Your appetite for food would be high. However, after you eat and are full, your appetite would decrease and if you eat too much it might make you sick. Money can work in the same way. That is why it is important to focus on all forms of wealth. Now I'm sure this will be different for everyone, and may depend on your culture or how you were raised. With that said, the important thing to remember is always be careful and cautious of what you are willing to sacrifice for Financial Wealth. Sacrificing your peace of mind, health, and even your freedom could be dangerous. What may seem like a means to an end, could ultimately result in a major loss. So, if happiness is your goal, focus on financial freedom and creating a lifestyle where you never have to worry about money again.

PHYSICAL WEALTH

Financial Wealth may be the most popular form of wealth, but Physical Wealth is easily the most important. Put simply, Physical Wealth is all about your health. I'm sure you have heard the saying "health is wealth", and the truth is health is the greatest wealth. That is because, without Physical Wealth obtaining or enjoying the other forms of wealth is impossible. Benjamin Franklin once said, "early to bed, early to rise, makes a man healthy wealthy and wise". So, if you really want to be "all about the Benjamins", it is important to invest in your health. Do not let illness make you realize the importance of your health. It is also important not to sacrifice your health for your lifestyle. Work to build habits that will support your health and grow Physical Wealth. This means incorporating exercise, nutrition, and rest in your daily routine. Remember, it's never too late to start investing in your health and putting it off will only cost you in the future. So do something today that your future self will thank you for. After all, what good is having money if you don't have the health to enjoy it?

SPIRITUAL WEALTH

Becoming Money Minded and shifting to a wealth mindset can be difficult at first. Today's world of social media and instant gratification has helped shape a culture of materialism and social comparison. With that said, now more than ever it is important to build a strong foundation of Spiritual Wealth. The essence of Spiritual Wealth is rooted in the mind and spirit. Spiritual Wealth can come in the form of mental health, education, or religion. Activities such as reading, therapy, meditation, and prayer can all help to grow your Spiritual Wealth. With an abundance of Spiritual Wealth, you will greatly improve your quality of life. You will also improve your ability to overcome stress, anxiety and other challenges life may bring. That said, if you are feeling pessimistic about life, take time to show gratitude for the good. If you are uneducated about something, dedicate time to learn. Take actions to improve your mental health and use that to create awareness of oneself. The best thing about Spiritual Wealth is it comes from within. It does not cost you anything to grow it, but the return on investment is priceless. All you need is time and someplace quiet to relax and think.

TIME WEALTH

Time is the most valuable asset you have. We have all heard the saying "time is money" and in many cases this is true. Think about working a 9 to 5. You are trading your 40 hours of time for a specific amount of money. When we talk, we say we spend time, or we spend money. Vice versa we say we save time, or we save money. You can start to see how time and money are correlated. The difference is you can get more money, but you can't get more time. That is why when you are young, you are rich with time. However, as you get older you will realize time is something you can never get back. The truth is, time is priceless and it is the ultimate currency. With that said, Time Wealth is about the appreciation of time and the creation of freedom. Most importantly the freedom to control how, when, where, and with whom you spend your time. In today's society creating Time Wealth can be challenging. The pursuit of Financial Wealth can create a constant cycle of trading time for money. For this reason, the best way to increase Time Wealth is to become financially free.

The goal of financial freedom is to create a lifestyle that does not require trading time for money. Unfortunately creating this type of lifestyle is often easier said than done. That is why obtaining financial freedom will require discipline and sacrifice. It will also force you to prioritize what is important in your life. Remember, there are only 24 hours in a day, and true Time Wealth means benefiting from every one of them. To do this you will need to find ways to make money even when you sleep. One way to do this is with passive income. Passive income is a major key to financial freedom and creating Time Wealth. Passive income is money that you earn automatically or with little effort. Some examples of passive income include rental income, interest income, or investment income. Learn to use passive income as a tool to grow your Time Wealth.

Another important key to increasing Time Wealth is also one of the simplest. You must stop wasting time. Like we said earlier, time is your most valuable asset. Unfortunately, procrastination is the thief of time. In a world of constant distraction, you must pay attention to how you spend your time. It is important to set goals and make them a priority in your life. Practice discipline and do your best to minimize nonproductive activities like social media, video games, and tv. I would also recommend waking up early. Research has shown that waking up early can reduce stress and improve your productivity. The key to Time Wealth will be rooted in your daily routine. Remember time wasted is life wasted.

SOCIAL WEALTH

There is a quote that says, "The real value of your wealth is how much you'd be worth if you lost all your money". When I hear this quote, I immediately think about Social Wealth. That is because Social Wealth is not about your net worth, it is about your network. Social Wealth is about your family, your friends, your colleagues, and your community. It is rooted in the quality of your relationships, the strength of your connections, and the time you have invested in others. The more positive social connections you have, the greater your Social Wealth. However, the more negative social connections you have the greater your social debt. To get the total value of your Social Wealth, simply add the value of your positive relationships and subtract the value of your negative ones. Remember no one is perfect, and you may experience positive and negative interactions with people. However, when assessing Social Wealth, the goal is for the good to outweigh the bad. Invest your time in people who are positive and supportive. Remove yourself from people who are dishonest and negative. That means you may have to let go of old friends and old ways. Regardless, focus on the strength of your relationships and not the length of your relationships. It is better to walk alone than with a crowd going in the wrong direction. The people you surround yourself with, will ultimately determine the growth of your Social Wealth. The saying "birds of a feather flock together" couldn't be more true. If you hang around four broke people, you are destined to be the fifth. With that said, if you hang around five millionaires, it won't be long before you are the sixth. Grow your Social Wealth and align yourself with people who have similar goals. With an abundance of Social Wealth, you will live confidently and improve your quality of life. Join a community, create a network, spend quality time with friends and family, and seek out positive influences and mentors. Always remember, your Social Wealth will not be about what you gain but what you give.

5 STEPS TO BECOME MONEY MINDED

1. Focus on wealth – The key to becoming Money Minded is to create a positive money mindset. With that said, the key to creating a positive money mindset is to focus on wealth. That means expanding your view of wealth to include not just Financial Wealth, but all forms of wealth. As we discussed earlier, there are five forms of wealth. These include Financial, Physical, Spiritual, Social, and Time Wealth. Each of these are equally important and will help shape your mindset. Work to create an abundance of all forms of wealth. This means if you are out of shape add exercise and nutrition to your daily routine. If your spirits are low, try reading, therapy, and prayer. If you can't find time to work on your goals, try cutting out social media, video games, and tv. Ultimately these activities will help to improve your quality of life and lay the foundation for becoming Money Minded.

2. Set goals– Life is full of distractions. When you consider family, friends, work, and school, it can be hard to prioritize what really matters. For this reason, setting realistic goals will be key to becoming Money Minded. Goals will help you focus and force you to identify what's most important. Working toward a goal that's important to you will give you the motivation to reach it. Setting goals is also a way to hold yourself accountable and measure your progress. If you have a big goal, try to break it down into smaller steps. As you accomplish each step, celebrate your achievements and reward yourself. A little progress each day can add up to big results. Remember, success in life is achieved by setting goals, taking action, and refusing to give up. If your plan isn't working, change your plan but don't change your goal. In the end what you will become in pursuit of your goals, will far outweigh the goals themselves.

3. Practice discipline and patience –In today's world of social media and instant gratification, patience and discipline are vital to becoming Money

Minded and shifting to a wealth mindset. In the previous section we discussed the importance of setting goals. That said, patience and discipline are key to reaching your goals and will act as a bridge between your goals and accomplishments. Remember, life is a marathon not a sprint. Success only happens over time and rarely overnight. Learn to use patience and discipline in place of motivation. That means doing what needs to be done, even when you don't feel like doing it. You will soon see that discipline will lead to habits, habits will lead to consistency, and consistency will lead to growth. For proof of this concept try using the 21/90 rule. The 21/90 rule says that doing something for 21 days straight will create a habit. If you continue doing it for 90 days, you will create a lifestyle. Making something a part of your lifestyle is the "ultimate discipline". Whether the goal is working out, saving money, or studying for an exam, use the 21/90 rule to help strengthen your patience and discipline.

4. Focus. Forgive. Forget. – Learning to focus,

forgive, and forget will be important in developing a Money Mindset. First when we say focus, we mainly mean focusing on yourself. Again, social media has created a space for people to display their highlights. Unfortunately, they rarely show the behind the scenes. Do not get in the habit of comparing yourself to others or as the saying goes "keeping up with the Joneses". Focus on your own path or risk getting lost following someone else's. Second, you must learn to forgive and forget. That means forgive yourself for past mistakes and forgive others for theirs. For example, maybe you were financially irresponsible in the past. Or maybe you cosigned a loan for a family member who ended up defaulting and hurting your credit score. Regardless of what it was, you must learn to forgive, forget, and move on. We all make mistakes in life, but holding ourselves hostage to these mistakes will ultimately prevent us from growing and moving forward. With that said, forget the mistake, but never forget what it taught you. Some of the most valuable lessons in life, especially financial, are learned by our mistakes and not by our triumphs.

5. Practice gratitude – One of the most important concepts to master in your journey to becoming Money Minded is the practice of gratitude. Gratitude is the expression of thankfulness and appreciation. It is about being grateful for where you are and what you have in life no matter how high or how low you may perceive yourself. There is an old saying that says "when you start counting your blessings, your blessings will start to count". This saying represents the essence of gratitude and is why gratitude is the foundation for all abundance. So, enjoy the little things in life because one day you will realize they are the big things. Cultivate a habit of being grateful and remember every good thing that comes to you should be returned with thanks. Practicing gratitude is magnetic and the more gratitude you show the more your abundance will grow.

CHAPTER TWO: WEALTH & HEALTH

In the last chapter we went over the five types of wealth. In this chapter we will take a closer look at the greatest form of wealth: Health. These days when people talk about investments, they often refer to real estate, stocks, or starting a business. For many it is difficult to understand that the most important investment you can make is actually in your health. For this reason, health is often viewed as an expense and not an investment. However, health is priceless making it the most valuable asset we own. Gandhi once said, "It is health that is real wealth and not pieces of gold and silver". That is because with health everything in your life will be amplified, including your finances. When your body is strong your mind will be strong. Together your mental and physical health will provide you with the energy, drive, and focus to pursue and accomplish your goals. Science has also shown a direct correlation between health and money. That is to say the healthier you are, the more money you will make. Conversely the more money you make, the healthier you will be. As we examine health and wealth, you will start to see the relationship between them. You will see how more of one helps the other and how less of one hurts the other. We will look at why healthier people have higher incomes, how your money affects your physical and mental health, and how to improve your health and money. Understanding these concepts will help you in your pursuit of Financial Wealth and help you establish a foundation for a long and fulfilling life.

HOW HEALTH IMPACTS INCOME

What if I told you healthy people earn more money and accumulate more wealth over their lifetime? What if I also told you healthy people save more money and have higher credit scores? Would this motivate you to be healthier? If not, it should, because all these things are true. Your health will have a direct effect on your finances. Not only will it help to prevent expensive health issues, but it could also affect your salary. Studies have proven that weight-based stereotypes are common. People viewed as obese or unhealthy are often categorized as lazy, unintelligent, and unreliable. In the end this leads to lower wages, less advancement opportunities, and higher unemployment. I've read studies that say an obese man can earn roughly $15,000 less per year when comparing to a healthy man in the same position. Over the course of a 40-year career, that could add up to more than a half-million dollars in lost earnings. Not to mention people who are obese have a shorter life expectancy. Research has shown men and women who are extremely obese, can anticipate their life expectancy will be reduced by an estimated 5 to 20 years. If you are a six-figure earner, losing 10 years of your life could cost you and your family millions in earned income. Now, consider a gym membership at a place like Planet Fitness would cost you about $10 per month. That adds up to be about $5,000 over the course of 40 years. If I told you an investment of $5,000 could get you upwards of $1.5 million, I'm sure you would want to know how. Well, you know the answer, and that is to take care of your health. With that said, below is a list of five other ways your health will impact your income.

5 WAYS HEALTH IMPACTS YOUR INCOME

1. Healthy people accumulate more Financial Wealth – It's really that simple. The healthier you are, the more money you will make. The examples above like salary and life expectancy are just some of the more obvious ways your health will directly affect your income and wealth. There are others like the rate at which healthy and unhealthy people invest. It was found that healthy people contribute more to their 401k than unhealthy people. Some say this is because healthy people have more of a "prevention mindset". This type of mindset ultimately leads to forward thinking and future planning. Put simply, healthy people expect to live long, while unhealthy people do not. Now this may not be a conscious decision but subconsciously when you live an unhealthy lifestyle that is what you are telling yourself. This can lead to poor financial decisions and create a "you only live once" mindset. That said, it would make since that unhealthy people account for a higher number of bankruptcies, foreclosures, and repossessions. They also have lower credit scores, smaller savings accounts, and bad breath. Ok, I was kidding about the bad breath, but you get the point. Your health will be key to growing Financial Wealth, and should be your number one investment.

2. Healthy people are more productive – There are only 24 hours in a day. When you have a family, a career, or your own business you must understand that every hour of the day is important. Being healthy will give you the energy to get the most out of your day. You'll be more productive and will save time. Remember, time is money. If you want to make more money, and don't have extra time, the best thing to do is be more productive with the time you have. That means less sleeping in, using fewer sick days, and taking less breaks. Why do you think employers have started to create incentives for weight loss, introduced exercise programs, and given employees access to fitness centers? They understand that healthier employees mean increased productivity and higher profits. Ultimately your goal is to work while they rest, learn while they party, and exercise while they sleep. Over time, an increase in your productivity will result in an increase to your bottom line.

3. Healthy people have more confidence – To be successful in your career or business, you must have self-confidence. Science has shown one of the best ways to increase self-confidence is through exercise and staying healthy. When you possess confidence, you possess value. However, without confidence you will be at a disadvantage. That is because having self-confidence means knowing your worth and understanding the value you offer. Have you noticed people who have confidence in business offer fewer discounts, close more deals, and charge more money? This is not because the product they offer is so much better. It is more about the confidence in how it is presented and ultimately how the customer perceives it. It also has a lot to do with how the customer perceives you. If you appear unhealthy and out of shape, not only will you feel less confident, but clients will perceive you that way. Studies have shown physical appearance affects a person's earning ability and we have already discussed the "fat penalty" for being overweight. By being physically fit, and having self-confidence you will have an advantage over the competition and grow your chances of increasing your income.

4. Healthy people take fewer sick days – This one is self-explanatory. Whether you work a 9 to 5 or run your own business, the less days you are sick the more days you could be working and making money. In fact, if you own your own business this is probably even more important. There is no sick leave for an entrepreneur. A week spent in bed sick can mean the difference between making a profit or taking a loss. Just think about what we saw with COVID. It was reported that millions of people are still suffering from "long COVID" and it has resulted in more than $160 billion in lost wages. That said, you start to see how important your health is to your income. I guess that's why they say, "it costs a little to be healthy, but it could cost you everything to be sick".

5. Healthy people spend less – There are only two ways to increase wealth. You can either make more or spend less. In the case of healthy people vs unhealthy people, healthy people spend less. Healthy people pay less for health services and medication. Healthy people also pay lower rates for life, health, and disability insurance. Now, it might seem obvious that healthy people would spend less on health care, but did you know they also spend less on clothes? It is estimated that "Big and Tall" sizes for men and "Plus-Size" clothing for women cost 10% to 15% more than average-size clothing. Diet can also affect your income. If you eat out a lot, or buy a lot of junk food, you may be spending more than if you were eating healthy. Not to mention healthy people tend to eat less, which can equate to a savings on their food bill. Another big savings can be found from cutting back on alcohol and smoking. Surveys have shown millennials spend an average of $300 a month on alcohol. If you add a $20 per day smoking habit, you are easily spending thousands annually on something that is only hurting your health. Again, saving money is the closest thing to making it. Save money by staying healthy and watch your income grow.

HOW WEALTH IMPACTS MENTAL AND PHYSICAL HEALTH

In the last section we discussed how your health impacts your Financial Wealth. In this section we will discuss how Financial Wealth impacts your health. Now this may seem like the same discussion, and it is true wealth and health have a paired relationship. However, wealth's impact on your mental and physical health is a very real thing. We have all heard the saying "more money, more problems". Nonetheless, I think we would all agree that not having enough money can pose an even bigger problem. I mean let's be real, you need money to survive. Not having money and a means for survival can have a real effect on your brain and ultimately your mental health. In fact, when your brain goes into survival mode for too long, you can even develop PTSD. Think about that. Being broke can actually drive you crazy. Not only that, it can create what doctors call our number one killer: stress. Research by the American Psychological Association (APA) found that money is the number one cause of stress in the United States. So, you can argue whether "money is the root of evil" but there is no argument that "money is the root of stress". Science has found that financial stress is responsible for a laundry list of mental and physical disorders. Studies show people with large amounts of debt are three times more likely to suffer from mental health problems like depression, anxiety, low self-esteem, and memory loss. Overtime, this creates a continued cycle of poor money habits which ultimately hurts your chances of improving your financial situation. Simply put, being broke can be a vicious cycle. Not only can it affect your mental health, but it can affect you physically too. Financial stress can lead to high blood pressure, heart disease, and immune disorders. It can also cause insomnia, headaches, and weight gain. People suffering financial stress have also been known to suffer from increased rates of alcoholism and drug use. Knowing this, you start to see how important it is to limit financial stress. Some of the best ways to prevent financial stress are to plan for the future, expect the unexpected, and do your best to live within your means. If you are faced with financial stress, don't ignore the problem, try to remain calm, and seek professional help if needed. Climbing out of a financial hole can be a challenge. Do your best to stay disciplined and protect your physical and mental health at all costs.

Now with that said, there is another side to the relationship between health and money. We have discussed how a lack of Financial Wealth can affect and harm our mental and physical health. However, an abundance of Financial Wealth can have the opposite effect. Now they say money can't buy happiness and technically money can't buy health. Nonetheless research has shown that the higher a person's income the better their health. This trend is consistent for both mental and physical health and across all income levels. For example, a person making between $35,000 and $50,000 annually, has roughly a 10.4% chance of suffering from diabetes. On the other hand, a person making $75,000 to $100,000 annually, has a 5.6% chance of developing diabetes. As you can see, something as small as a $25,000 increase in your annual salary could cut your chances of developing diabetes almost in half. The fact is, this is not just true for diabetes, this is also true for kidney disease (1.9% vs .9%), liver disease (1.6% vs .6%), emphysema (2.5% vs 1%), and a host of other health conditions. For most, the fact that wealthy people are healthier than poor people is not much of a surprise. Wealthier people have better access to health care, clean water, fresh produce, and healthier food options. Not only that, advertisers also target low-income and minority communities for unhealthy products like, tobacco, alcohol, and fast food. Couple this with the mental health impact of poverty, and you can see why the health gap between rich and poor continues to grow. Again, this section is not to point out the obvious, but to serve as a reminder. A reminder that the relationship between income and health is real and they are connected on every level of the economic ladder. Always remember this on your journey to financial freedom. Understanding the relationship between wealth and health will help you build a lifestyle of prosperity, strength, and abundance.

HOW TO IMPROVE YOUR HEALTH AND MONEY

The healthier you are the more money you will make. The more money you make the healthier you will be. This is the cycle of wealth. As you know wealth isn't all about your bank account. Wealth is about balance. Largely, wealth is about balance between financial abundance and physical and spiritual abundance. That means to improve your health and money you must focus on activities that incorporate all aspects of wealth. That said, this does not mean go create a to-do list of health and wealth goals. What this means is you should first focus on your lifestyle. Financial, Physical, and Spiritual Wealth only exists when a person's daily pursuits allow them to grow. Put simply, your success will be found in your daily routine. If you go to the gym a couple times a week, but eat fast food every day, you can't really expect to get healthier. Just like the person who gets a raise at work but then decides to go buy a more expensive car can't expect to get wealthier. The bottom-line is you can't expect a harvest if you don't plant the seeds. Creating or changing your lifestyle will be the key to planting those seeds and simultaneously improving your health and money. Below is a list of five lifestyle mindsets that can be used to achieve this goal.

5 LIFESTYLE MINDSETS TO IMPROVE YOUR HEALTH AND MONEY

1. Live within your means – This is one of the most important things you can do to provide balance and improve both your health and money. To live within your means is to be financially responsible. It means each month you should be spending less than you make or at least equal to what you make. There is a quote by Warren Buffett that says, "Do not save what is left after spending, but spend what is left after saving". This is the essence of a "living within your means" mindset. It is also the key to financial abundance. With that said, some people are often skeptical of a "living within your means" mindset. They say it limits creativity and it teaches you a scarcity mindset. The problem with that line of thinking is numbers don't lie. If you consistently spend more than you make, you will end up in debt. Not only that, the health risks associated with financial stress are far more concerning than any "scarcity mindset". The truth is, if you want to live beyond your current means, work to expand them. That means find a side hustle, invest in a business, or find a higher paying job. Remember abundance is less about the money and more about freedom. Creating a lifestyle that is consistent with your means will provide you with the freedom, flexibility, and focus to improve both your health and money.

2. Exercise and stay active – The benefits of exercise are well known as it relates to health. Exercise protects you from heart disease, reduces the risk of diabetes, lowers blood pressure, and decreases the risk of cancer. It also reduces stress and combats anxiety and depression. But did you know exercise can improve your finances? That is because exercise sharpens your memory and improves focus. Subsequently, this helps you learn faster and increases your productivity. Achieving and maintaining high levels of productivity is essential to financial success. The more productive you are, the more promotions, salary increases, and bonuses you will receive. The more productive your business, the more products you can produce and the more clients you can service. In the end, exercise will enhance health, health will enhance productivity, and productivity will enhance income.

3. Plan ahead – They say proper planning prevents poor performance. When it comes to your health and finances, this statement could not be more true. It is important to plan ahead and be prepared not only for emergencies but also for opportunities. In terms of health, we've talked about the benefits of exercise and staying active. However, it is also important to take preventative steps regarding your health. This means scheduling regular doctor visits and ensuring you have adequate health coverage. As you get older, proper health planning will become increasingly important. I recommend creating a personal health or wellness plan to track your goals and progress. You can also include your financial goals as a part of the plan. Remember financial planning is equally important. Doing things like creating an emergency fund and saving for retirement are vital tasks that should be added to any financial plan. It is also wise to plan and save for any large purchases like a car or your first home. Whatever the goal, a financial plan will be helpful. Plan today for a successful tomorrow and watch your health and finances flourish.

4. Watch what you put in your body – There is an old proverb that says "tell me what you eat, and I'll tell you what you are". This is because your diet is more than just what you eat. Your diet is also what you watch, what you listen to, and what you read. When you understand this, you begin to see how important it is to watch what you put in your body. Remember, your body and mind will become what you consume. If you eat unhealthy food, you will be unhealthy. If you listen to negativity, you will have negative thoughts. It's really that simple. If your plan is to obtain physical and financial abundance, make sure you create an environment that will allow them to grow. This means consuming nutritious foods, reading for education, and surrounding yourself with people who love and support you. This also means avoiding negative tv programing, curbing your time on social media, and limiting the amount of depressing or violent music you listen to. By doing these things, and being more mindful of what you consume, you will have the groundwork for cultivating health and income.

5. Learn to do it yourself – When people hear "do-it-yourself", they often think of home repair or renovations. However, the "do-it-yourself" mindset is more about being self-sufficient and independent. It is also about problem solving and self-education. As you work to improve your health and income, applying the "do-it-yourself" mindset will be key. In terms of finances the obvious benefit for employing the "do-it-yourself" mindset is the cash savings. I personally have saved tens of thousands of dollars applying this mindset. Simply put, why pay someone for something you can do yourself? Not only that, you may gain a skill that can be used to generate income in the future.

In terms of health, the "do-it-yourself" mindset is also beneficial. For example, a basic skill to learn would be how to cook and prepare healthy meals. This will help you maintain a nutritious diet and save you time and money eating out. I would also recommend learning a basic workout routine. Staying in shape does not require a gym membership or a personal trainer. Learn skills that will help you become more self-sufficient when it comes to maintaining your health. In the end practicing a "do-it-yourself" mindset will help you improve your health and money.

CHAPTER THREE: BUDGET & SAVINGS

What is budgeting? - When it comes to money, budgeting is a life tool. Budgeting is the simplest and most effective way to manage your money. With that said, budgeting takes discipline and a money mind to be successful. Budgeting will also require patience, but with time you can make it a useful tool in your financial toolbox.

5 REASONS TO START A BUDGET

1. Numbers don't lie – A budget will give you a TRUE picture of your financial position. It will help you identify what you are spending your money on and how much you are spending. It will also help you understand what you can truly afford. Unfortunately, you may find that the truth hurts. That said, it is always better to "know what you have, before blowing a bag". Always control your money and never let your money control you. Having a budget will save you from stressing over where your money went, and why you don't have enough to pay your bills. It can be depressing putting the numbers on paper, especially if you have more going out than you have coming in. Regardless, you must do this if you really want to take control of your finances and obtain financial freedom.

2. Keeps you focused and disciplined – Saving money takes discipline. Creating a budget will force you to focus on your financial goals. Review and update your budget weekly. This will help you avoid spending on unnecessary stuff. It will also help you identify any possible money problems in advance. If you spot an issue or fall off track, try to make adjustments so that you can meet your monthly goals. If you are working with a tight budget, it is even more important to remain disciplined. When it comes to budgeting and savings, patience plus time is the only way to reach success.

3. Turn expenses to income – There are only two ways to have more money. Make more or spend less. With budgeting, you can see what is coming in and what is going out. If you use your budget correctly you can find ways to turn expenses to income. Every dollar you stop from going out is the same as a new dollar coming in. Try to find expenses that can be cut and turned into savings. This is one of the quickest ways to generate additional cash flow. Why do you think when businesses are struggling, the first thing they do is layoff people or close underperforming stores. It's because shedding expenses will immediately impact your bottom line and increase income.

4. Predict the future - A budget will help you predict and plan for the future. In some ways a budget can act as your personal business plan, and a tool that can be used to accomplish your goals. If you are trying to save for your first home, a budget will tell you how long it's going to take. It's simple, say you need to save $10,000 for a down payment on a house. If you are able to save $1000 per month, you'll reach your goal in 10 months. If you can only save $100 per month, it's going to take you over 8 years. You don't have to be a fortune teller to see how a budget can predict your future. Remember there are no shortcuts when it comes to budgeting and saving. Patience and discipline are the only ways to be successful. Do your future self a favor and start saving now.

5. Keeps you ready – Have you ever heard the saying "stay ready so you don't have to get ready"? This is definitely a cash rule and budgeting will make sure you are following it. Opportunities or obstacles in life often come when least expected. Make sure you are always prepared for them. Even if you don't have a specific goal, use your budget to set aside money in case something happens. There is nothing worse than missing an opportunity because you were not ready to make a move. There is also nothing worse than having an emergency, and you don't have the money to fix it. Keeping a budget will ensure you are aware of your current financial position and give you insight into where you will be in the future.

Bonus - Save your marriage – This is for those of you in a relationship. If you share your money with your spouse or partner, a budget is critical. A budget can help communicate how money is being spent and who is spending what. Most importantly creating a budget will reduce conflicts and help to resolve differences in how the money is spent. Budgeting can also promote teamwork and ensure each person is being held accountable. Money is the one thing that can tear a relationship apart. Make sure you address it early and use a budget to communicate clearly your financial position and goals.

HOW TO CREATE A BUDGET AND SAVE

1. Put all your cards on the table – The first step when starting a budget is to write down EVERYHTING. That means all the money you are spending and all the money you are making. I would recommend using the prior month as an example. List out all of your expenses starting with the biggest. This might include rent, mortgage, car payments, insurance, utilities, credit cards, student loans, groceries and etc. Write them all down and enter the amounts. If it's something that fluctuates month to month, like some utilities, then overestimate the amounts. Try to capture as much as you can. If you are noticing a bunch of random one-time expenses, just add them up and put them under miscellaneous. Even though they seem like a onetime expense, do not fail to budget for them. Trust me, there will always be something to take its place.

2. Necessity or accessory – Once you have laid

out all of your spending, it's time to prioritize your budget. To do this look at each item in your budget and ask yourself is this a necessity or an accessory. For example, your rent or mortgage is definitely a necessity. Your electric and water bill would also be considered necessities. In today's world a cell phone would also be a necessity, but technically you could survive without it. Your cable bill, especially Wi-Fi, may also be a necessity, but the HBO and Starz package might be considered accessories. I understand this can be difficult. For some people a vacation is a necessity, and to others going out to eat is a necessity. It is really up to you how you prioritize your spending and your life. The most important part is that at the end of each month you have enough to cover all your expenses. With that said, if you add up all your necessities and accessories and they total more than your monthly income, STOP and go back through your list. You may be forced to make some hard decisions, but one of the first steps to financial freedom is living below your means.

3. Prioritize and strategize – Now that you have laid out your financial picture, it's time to prioritize and strategize. To do this you must first ask yourself what your goal is. Having a goal will provide you with the motivation, focus, and discipline needed to stick to your budget. Having a goal will also help you determine the best strategy for reaching it. Remember there are only two ways to have more money. Make more or spend less. Depending on the goal you are trying to reach, it could be as simple as cutting some accessory expenses. However, if you are reaching for a larger goal, you may need to find a way to make more money. Either way, create a strategy that is realistic and most importantly one you can stick to. It is ok to adjust your budget, but it is not ok to give up.

4. Pay your goal first – Once you have decided on a goal, it's important to pay your goals first. That means if your goal is to pay an extra $200 per month on your Student Loan, then pay it using your first check. Get it out of the way. You will save yourself the temptation of spending that money by taking care of your goals first. You can also use autopay or direct deposit to make payments or savings much easier. You should also open at least two accounts. One to spend from and one for saving. Whatever account you use for saving, make sure the money is not easy to access. This means do not attach a debit card to the account. If there is a debit card attached to it, make sure you leave the card at home and don't carry it with you. The harder it is for you to spend, the easier it will be to stick to your budget.

5. Patience & follow up – Budgeting and saving is not a get rich quick philosophy. However, if you stick to it, budgeting is 100% successful. With that said, you must have patience. Give yourself time to see the results. I understand this can be easier said than done, but without patience a budget won't work. To help you stay focused, try to break up your goal. I like to break mine up into four quarters and pretend like it's a game. Also make sure you are checking your progress at least monthly. It is easier to make adjustments early rather than letting them compound. Always pay your goals first and reward yourself when you reach a milestone.

You will be surprised how fast the time will go, and even more surprised with the results.

CHAPTER FOUR: CREDIT

What Is credit? – On your path to FINANCIAL FREEDOM, the first roadblock that you may encounter is credit. So, whether that's getting your first credit card, buying a car, or purchasing your first home, you will most likely need credit. Credit is simply your ability to buy now and pay later. I used to have a joke that I would use anytime someone would ask me to buy something. I would respond "Sure… I'll buy… you pay". Everyone would look confused at first, but eventually they would get the point. Buying and paying are two different things. Having credit will allow you to buy stuff and use your credit to pay for them. As you can imagine, there are benefits to being able to buy something, even if you don't have the cash to pay for it. With that said, nothing in life is free. Using and managing credit takes discipline. Always make sure you understand the terms. Not knowing when and how much you will have to pay later can be a costly mistake. It is already hard enough to obtain credit, and it takes work to maintain it. Unfortunately, it is also easy to lose it. That is why understanding how credit works will be a major key to credit success.

WHAT IS YOUR CREDIT SCORE

They say numbers don't lie; and when it comes to your credit score the numbers won't try. Put simply, it is what it is. If you have a 500-credit score, you can't tell the bank it's because you lost your job, or your cousin stopped making payments on that Dodge Charger you co-signed for. The only thing you can do is fix the issue, and to fix the issue you must understand how your score is calculated. Your credit score is calculated based on five key elements and can range from 300 to 850 points. The five key elements of your credit score are payment history (35%), how much money you owe (30%), credit history (15%), types of credit (10%), and age of credit (10%). Each one of these factors will play a role in your current credit score. Improving each of these areas can also help to improve your score. With that said, here are some steps you can take to improve your credit score.

6 STEPS TO IMPROVING YOUR CREDIT SCORE

1. Get a copy of your credit reports – This may seem obvious, but you would be surprised by how many people have never pulled their credit reports. Some people are also surprised to know they have three credit reports. That's one for each of the three credit bureaus (Equifax, Experian, and Transunion). You can get copies of all three credit reports free of charge at AnnualCreditReport.com.

Before you can fix your credit, you must know what is on your reports. Your credit reports are a record of your payment history, account balances, credit history, and credit inquiries. Make sure you review everything in the reports and ensure they are accurate. Errors on your reports can lower your score, so it is very important to get this information removed.

2. Dispute credit report errors – If you find errors on your credit report, you should dispute it with the credit reporting companies (Experian, Equifax, and/or Transunion). Under the Fair Credit Reporting Act, credit reporting companies must investigate the dispute within 30 days. If the investigation is not completed or the creditor fails to respond within the 30 days, the information must be removed. Disputes can be filed online. Your dispute should explain in writing the error and include copies of documents that support your dispute. Disputing and removing derogatory credit information is one of the quickest ways to improve your credit score. Below are links to dispute errors online for each of the credit reporting companies (Experian, Equifax, and/or Transunion).

Equifax Online:

www.equifax.com/personal/credit-report-services/credit-dispute/

Experian Online:

www.experian.com/disputes/main.html

TransUnion Online:

https://dispute.transunion.com

3. Make your payments – As we discussed earlier, your payment history makes up the largest part of your score calculation. This means 35% of your credit score is determined by whether or not you are making your payments on time. Late payments can destroy your credit score. If you are behind on payments, you must work to get them current. If your payments are current, do whatever you can to keep them current. If you have a hard time remembering due dates, I recommend using some sort of autopay to ensure you pay on time. If you have a credit card, make sure you are making at least the minimum payment. Simply making your payments on time will greatly improve your credit score.

4. Keep your balances low – The amount of money that you owe is the second largest factor in determining your credit score. This is called your credit utilization and it makes up 30% of your credit score. The way credit utilization works is it takes the total credit you have available and compares it to how much you are using. You can calculate it by dividing what you owe by your credit limit. For example, if your credit limit is $1000 and you have spent or owe $500, your credit utilization is 50%. Having a utilization percentage over 30% can begin to hurt your credit score. That is why it is never good to max-out a credit card. Especially if it is your only credit card. With that said, if you have high balances, you must find a way to pay them down. Even better, try not to create the balance in the first place. Being disciplined with your spending is important and you should always try to pay off your balances at the end of each month. This will ensure your utilization stays low and will also save you money on interest.

5. Credit inquires - Applying for new credit will create a "hard inquiry" on your credit report. Hard inquiries make up 10% of your credit score Too many inquiries can decrease your score. Be disciplined when applying for credit. That 20% off they are offering to apply for a Macy's card, could cost you points on your credit score.

6. Patience and discipline – Patience and discipline aren't used to calculate your credit score, but you will need them to fix your credit. There are no shortcuts when it comes to improving your credit. Credit repair companies and credit "gurus" aren't doing anything you can't do for yourself. Be cautious of people who tell you they can fix your credit for a fee. You may be better off using that money to make a payment or pay down a balance.

BENEFITS OF GOOD CREDIT

Good credit can make your financial life easier. Good credit can help you get a mortgage, an apartment, or a car. Good credit has lots of benefits, but the most important one is that it can save you money. I like to say good credit is like having a financial EZ pass. It will allow you to travel the financial highway without having to stop and pay the tolls. But when we are talking about credit, the tolls we are talking about is the interest or the interest rate. Interest is the toll for borrowing money. The better your credit the less interest you will pay. The less interest you pay the more money you will save.

THREE WAYS YOUR CREDIT SCORE SAVES YOU MONEY

1. Lower interest rates – The #1-way good credit saves you money is with lower interest rates. Let's look at a real life example of how good credit and lower interest rates can save you money.

Let's say you apply for a 7-year $25,000 auto loan. Having good credit could qualify you for a 3.5% interest rate. Your monthly payment would be about $455, and you'd pay $2,300 in interest over the five years.

However, if you have bad credit, you could pay a rate closer to 13.5%. At this rate your monthly payment would be around $575, and you'd pay $9,500 in interest over the five years. So, with good credit you would save almost $125 on your monthly payment and $7,200 over the course of five years. That's a lot of money to save for the same car and just for having good credit.

2. Credit card offers & bonuses – Once you establish good credit you will begin to qualify for special credit card offers and bonuses. One of my favorites is the 0% interest introductory offer. I wouldn't even apply for a card that didn't have a 0% interest introductory offer. With this offer, you don't pay interest on charges for a set period, sometimes a year or more. Granted, you have to pay off the balance before the end of the intrest free period. However, for a year the card is interest free. I like to do what I call a credit card relay. I will pay off my balances right before the end of the interest free period and then apply for a new card that offers 0% interest. Using the credit card relay, I haven't paid interest on a credit card in over 10 years. Remember you have to pay off the balance before the end of the interest free period. If you are not disciplined with your spending, you could be on the hook for interest on any balance that's remaining.

Cash bonuses are another way to save money on

credit cards. For example, I have received offers for a $200 bonus for spending as little as $500. That's a 40% discount. I know my cell phone and cable bill are almost $500 per month. In this case, I would pay them both with the credit card and get a free $200. Just like the 0% interest introductory offer, I rarely apply for cards that don't include some sort of cash bonus or rewards.

3. Bank account bonuses – Just like with credit card bonuses, banks will offer you money just to open an account with them. I just received an offer for $325 if you have direct deposit for 90 days. Most companies will allow you to have direct deposits to multiple accounts. If you don't want all of your money to go to this account, just set it up so enough of it does to qualify for the bonus. After you receive the bonus, you are free to close the account and pursue the next offer. You could easily receive $1000 or more over the course of a year doing this. However, there are only so many banks. Once you have received a bonus from a bank, they may make you wait at least a year before you can

receive another one.

PART II: ASSETS & LIABILITIES

In the second part of the book, we are going to go over assets & liabilities. We will touch on real estate, cars, investments, starting your own business, and more.

CHAPTER FIVE: REAL ESTATE

Most of us have heard the term real estate. But did you know the real estate industry is the biggest industry in the United States? Did you also know the U.S. Constitution used to require you to own real estate just to vote? That said, you can see how important real estate is, especially in the United States. Real estate is a gateway to wealth and may be the first investment you make in life. Yes, buying a home is an investment. With that said, there are several types of real estate. The most common is residential real estate. Residential real estate can include single-family homes, condominiums, townhouses, multi-family, and vacation homes. The next type of real estate is commercial real estate. Commercial real estate can include apartment buildings, shopping centers, hotels, and offices. Lastly, there is industrial real estate. Industrial real estate would include places like factories and warehouses. All of these different types of real estate make up the trillion dollar real estate industry. In most cases your first experience with real estate will be with residential real estate and buying a home. Because of this, we will primarily focus on residential real estate in this chapter.

HOW REAL ESTATE WORKS

The residential real estate industry is made up of three key groups. These groups include buyers and sellers, real estate agents, and banks.

Buyers and Sellers

Buyers and sellers can be people like you and I looking to buy their first home or sell the one they have. You also have investors who buy and sell homes as a business. I'm sure you have heard the term flipping houses. This is when an investor buys a home and resells it for more after fixing it up. Banks can also be home sellers, but we will talk more about that later.

Real Estate Agents

Next you have real estate agents. Real estate agents help buyers and sellers buy and sell property. A sellers agent would list the property for sale and help find buyers. They will help set the price of the property, using recently sold homes called "comparable," or "comps. They may help stage the property and set up an open house for potential buyers. Once they get a buyer, the seller's agent will assist in negotiations and help to get the highest price possible.

Buyers' agents help buyers purchase properties. They can help find a property that meets your needs and set up showings so that you can view them. Buyers' agents will also help negotiate price and submit a purchase offer. Once an offer is accepted, they can also help set up a property inspection and appraisal. A buyers agent can also work with you to obtain financing from a bank or lender.

A good real estate agent should be able to walk you through the buying and selling process from start to finish. For their services real estate agents are paid a commission once the deal is done. The average commission is 3% of the sale or purchase price.

Banks

The last key group in the real estate industry is

banks. Banks provide money for buyers to purchase real estate. This is done by using what is called a mortgage. Roughly 70% of homes are bought using a mortgage. A mortgage allows qualified buyers to purchase property for as little as 3.5% of the purchase price. We will talk more about how to qualify for a mortgage later in this chapter. Once the bank issues the mortgage, the buyer will be required to make monthly payments for the term of the loan. Most first-time home buyers start with a 30 year mortgage. The property will then act as collateral against the loan. This means if the buyer fails to pay the mortgage, the bank has the right to repossess the property. The process of repossession is called foreclosure. We mentioned earlier that banks can also be sellers of property. Foreclosed or bank owned properties provide some of the best opportunities for buyers looking to enter the real estate market.

INVESTING IN REAL ESTATE

Anyone who buys or sells real estate is a real estate investor. This means if you are buying a home to live in, to use as a rental or Airbnb, or to fix and flip, always look at the purchase as an investment. Real estate investments, just like any other investments, come with risk and it is important to do your due diligence. I like to call this giving the property a lie detector or L.I.A.R test. To give a property a L.I.A.R. test we focus on four key elements. These elements consist of **L**ocation, **I**nspection, **A**ppraisal, and **R**ules (L.I.A.R.).

L.I.A.R.

Location

Location is one of the most important factors to consider when deciding to buy real estate. This is because location is the one feature that can't be changed or duplicated. When judging location, always ask yourself "what can I get to in 10 min if I decide to jump in my car or call an Uber?". Then ask yourself "what can I get to in 30 min?". Are you close to the water or one of the areas main attractions? In 30 minutes can you reach downtown or the cities center? Typically, the closer you are to employment centers, shopping, entertainment, and recreation, the more valuable the location will be. Next, look to see how close you are to transportation. This means freeways, train stations, and airports. Access to transportation hubs is always key when considering location. Especially in today's world when long commutes are becoming less and less desirable. Other areas buyers may want to consider are the school system, crime rates, and the neighborhood's status or reputation. With that said, the recent trend of gentrification has proven these characteristics can change fast. With any investment the goal is to get in low before the prices get high. Look for real estate in locations that are trending up. Remember neighborhoods can change but location won't.

Inspection

Once you have checked out the location, the next step is the inspection. Inspection put simply is checking the condition of the property. Has the property been recently renovated or remodeled? Is the property unlivable? The condition of the property will always affect the price someone is willing to pay for it. If the property is in great condition, you can expect to pay top dollar. However, if the property is in poor condition, you may be able to get it at a discount. In my opinion, a discount on a property in poor condition is better than a premium on a house in good condition. Especially if you have the time and resources to fix it up. We will talk about the reason why when we talk about flipping houses. The bottom-line is to make sure to inspect the property and confirm its condition before buying.

Appraisal

The next part of our L.I.A.R. test is appraisal. Appraisal is when you estimate the value of the property. If you are using a mortgage to buy a property, the bank will require an appraisal. However, before you get to that step you should be doing your own appraisal. Once you have completed the first two steps of evaluating the location and inspecting the property, it shouldn't be hard to come up with an estimate of the property's value. No appraisal is exact and yours doesn't have to be either. The primary purpose is to answer one question. Is the price of this property worth it? One of the biggest mistakes in real estate is overpaying for a property. To get started on your personal appraisal, go to a website like Zillow or Redfin. Next search for properties that have sold recently in that location. This is called finding comps or comparables. If you find similar properties that have sold for more or close to the list price, you can feel comfortable that the property is worth it. Always make sure to consider the square footage and condition when looking at comps. Again, you are only trying to get an estimate of the property's value.

Rules

The final step is to research the "rules" associated with the property. People always ask me what this means and are unaware that many properties come with rules that must be followed. Have you ever heard of an HOA or a condo association? What about zoning? Depending on the location, a property may have restrictions that govern what can and can't be done with the property. For example, some HOA's won't allow you to use the property for Airbnb. Others may limit the number of vehicles you can have. If the property is in a residential zone, you may not be able to turn it into a duplex. All of these different "rules" can impact your potential investment. Make sure you research the rules before moving forward with any real estate purchase.

Giving a potential real estate investment a lie detector or L.I.A.R test will help you separate opportunities from mistakes. Each opportunity will come with different challenges, but Location, Inspection, Appraisal, and Rules will always play a part. You will see the benefits as we look at some of the most popular types of real estate investments.

BUYING A HOME

In most cases, buying a home will be your first experience with real estate investing. Buying a home is a big decision and can also be a big accomplishment. However, buying a home is different than other real estate investments. In fact, some people say it is not an investment at all. But trust me, it is. The difference is some people treat buying a home as a luxury rather than an investment. The truth is it can be both. You must ask yourself why you are buying a home and make a decision if this is going to be an investment or a luxury. To do this consider two things. First, what is the condition of the property? Is it something you are going to fix up, or is it new construction? Remember a discount on a property in poor condition is better than a premium on a house in good condition. This is because you can gain equity by fixing up a home. Equity is the difference between what a property cost and what it is worth. We have all seen the HGTV shows where they spend 250k to buy and fix up a house, but then the house is worth 300k. That extra 50k is equity. Going into a home with equity is the best way to guarantee you earn a return on your investment. The second thing to consider is how long do you plan to stay in the home? If the answer is less than 3 years, I would consider this a luxury purchase. The longer you stay in a home, the more equity you will build and the greater the chance the home will appreciate. This means the chances you will see a return on your investment will increase. Also, if you stay in a home for at least 3 years, you can avoid taxes on any potential profits. I'm not saying it's impossible to make a return in under 3 years, but the chances are much less, and the return will probably be much smaller. Especially if you are buying a new construction or recently renovated property.

STEPS TO BUYING A HOME

Run the numbers - When it comes to buying a home it's all about the numbers. Whether it's your credit score, income, debt to income ratio, or your down payment, these are all numbers you need to know.

First start with your credit score. The higher your credit score, the better chance you have to get approved for a mortgage. FHA loans usually require a score of 580 or higher. A score of 720 or higher will allow you to qualify for a conventional loan. We'll talk more about the difference between an FHA loan and a conventional loan when we discuss financing. The bottom line is knowing your score before you apply. The better your credit score the lower your interest rate. When it comes to mortgages, a low interest rate is what it's all about. If you have questions about your credit score and how to improve it make sure you read Chapter 4.

The next numbers to know are your income and most importantly your debt-to-income ratio or DTI. Your DTI is your monthly expenses divided by your gross monthly income. Your monthly expenses would include rent, car payments, student loans, child support, and credit card payments etc.. Basically, anything that would show up on a credit report. Expenses like utilities, childcare, and groceries would not be included. For income simply take your Gross monthly income. Gross income is the amount you earn before taxes and insurance are taken out. Make sure you have check stubs or tax returns to support your income. Banks take income verification very seriously. Let's look at an example. Say you pay $1500 a month for rent, $300 a month for a car payment, and $200 for credit cards. Your monthly expenses would be $2,000 ($1500 + $300 + $200 = $2,000). If your gross monthly income is $5,000, then your debt-to-income ratio is 40% ($2,000 divided by $5,000). Banks like your DTI to be under 43%. In this example the $1500 that you are paying for rent is close to what your mortgage payment would need to be. With that said, make sure you know your income and DTI before you start the home buying process.

The last number you need to know is that number under balance in your bank account. Yes, buying a home will take some cash even if you are using a mortgage to buy it. Most banks require a down payment for a mortgage. You will also have to put down a deposit with your offer to purchase a home. I would recommend saving a minimum of 5% of the purchase price for the home. So, if you want to buy a $300,000 home, you need to save at least $15,000. With that said, it's possible to get a loan with less than 5% down, and there are programs out there that can help with down payment assistance and closing costs. Regardless, I would still recommend saving the money. Buying a home is a big responsibility, and if you end up having extra money it will only help you in the long run.

Start a watch list – Once you have your numbers, it's time to start your watch list. Your watch list should be a list of neighborhoods or zip codes that have homes in your budget. You can start by going to www.redfin.com or www.zillow.com. Do a general search for homes in your price range. Try to get an idea of the types of homes and locations that interest you. If you find a home in a location you are not familiar with, I recommend doing a "drive by" to check out the area. You can also use street view, but nothings better than seeing it for yourself. Remember, you will have to prioritize your watch list. Your budget will likely determine the size, location, and amenities you can afford. With that in mind, make sure you identify what's most important to you in a home.

Call the professionals – At this point you should have an idea of what you can afford and the location and type of home you are looking for. Now would be a good time to contact a real estate agent. In most cases, especially for a buyer, having an agent is a no brainer. That's because the seller of whatever property you buy is going to pay your agent's commission. For a home buyer having an agent costs you nothing. At least not in the form of a fee. With that said, make sure you are comfortable with your agent. You want to make sure they are knowledgeable and are going to act quickly and professionally on your behalf. In today's market, homes are selling quicker than ever. Your agent may have to act fast in order for you to be successful in buying a home. A good agent will also have relationships with lenders, home inspectors, and contractors that can help you along the way.

Get pre-approved – Most people don't pay all cash for a home. So, if you are most people you will need to get a mortgage. The first step in getting a mortgage and buying a home is "pre-approval". A pre-approval is a process in which a bank or lender will review your income, debt, and credit history. Based on this initial review, the bank will "pre-approve" you for a set amount and interest rate. This approval will usually come in the form of a letter called a pre-approval letter. When you submit an offer for a home, you would also include this preapproval letter to show the seller you have the ability to purchase the home. It is important to have your documents together before applying for a pre-approval. These documents should include your pay statements, W2s or 1099s, tax returns, and bank statements. If you have any other income that you would like them to consider, make sure you have documents to prove these amounts as well. Remember, you don't have to use the same bank to finance your loan that you used for your pre-approval. You should always get estimates from multiple banks to compare interest rates and fees before actually committing to a bank.

Seek & Destroy – The next step in the home buying process is to Seek & Destroy. I know you're asking yourself what Seek and Destroy is. Simply put, Seek & Destroy is the process of finding a home you like and getting the seller to accept your offer. To some it may sound harsh, but in today's market this is the mentality you must have to get a property under contract. The Seek & Destroy mentality means you should be looking at listings daily. When you find a listing that fits your criteria, you should schedule a showing ASAP. During the showing make sure to view the entire property inside and out. Keep an eye out for structural issues like cracks in walls or uneven floors. You also want to view the condition of the appliances and HVAC systems. Some other things you can do are check water pressure by turning on faucets, make sure the light switches work, check if the doors and windows open smoothly, and check the neighboring properties condition. Don't worry if you don't catch everything. You will have a chance to do a professional inspection once the property is under contract. After viewing the property, make sure to give it the L.I.A.R test. If it passes the test, you should consider making an offer. You shouldn't make an offer unless you are sure this is the home for you. However, don't wait too long to decide because you could also miss the opportunity.

Make an offer they can't refuse – Making an offer on a home can be a confusing and stressful process. Especially in today's market when homes are going under contract fast and selling over the asking price.

There is a strong chance you will only have one shot at making an offer so you must make an offer the seller can't refuse. In order to make an offer they can't refuse you must consider several things.

The first thing to consider is price. Ask yourself what is the highest amount you would pay for the property. Not to say you have to offer your highest and best from the jump, but remember if your offer is too low you could miss your chance. If you have given it the L.I.A.R test you should know what comparable homes are selling for in the area. I also recommend looking at how many days the house has been on the market. If it has been on the market for longer than 15 days, there is a strong chance you could offer list price or slightly below list. If you are making an offer during the first 15 days on the market, you should consider an offer at the list price or slightly over. Again, we are in a sellers' market. If we move to a buyers' market, then offers under the list price would have a stronger chance of being accepted.

The second thing to consider are the

contingencies. A contingency is an agreement within the contract that says certain things must happen before the sale can close. Some common contingencies are the inspection contingency, appraisal contingency, and the finance contingency. In real estate the less contingencies you have in your contract, the stronger the offer will be for the seller.

The inspection contingency is one of the most common and most important contingencies in a real estate contract. The inspection contingency says you get to have a professional inspection before you buy the home. If after the inspection you want out of the contract, you would be released and receive your deposit back. I would recommend you have an inspection contingency in your contract. However, in a sellers' market many buyers forego an inspection in an effort to make their offer stronger. Sellers like this because it can shorten the time it takes to close and can prevent buyers from asking for repairs or reductions in the offer price.

Another common contingency is the finance

contingency. The finance contingency says that if the buyer is not approved for a mortgage, then they are released from the purchase contract. This contingency is standard for buyers using a mortgage to finance their home purchase. However, it is also why you often hear of buyers with cash offers beating out buyers who are using a mortgage to finance the purchase. A cash buyer would not have a finance contingency because they are not financing the purchase. Sellers favor cash offers because they can close quickly and there are less chances the deal will fall through. If you have the means to make a cash offer and eliminate the finance contingency, there is as strong chance you will be able to make an offer they can't refuse.

The last common contingency is the appraisal contingency. The appraisal contingency states the house must appraise for the selling price or above. Again, buyers may forego this contingency in an effort to make their offer stronger. However, if you are taking out a mortgage to buy the property, the bank may require an appraisal contingency. If the bank does not require the appraisal contingency, they may only loan you an amount up to the appraised value of the property. For example, if you offer $300,000 for the home and it only appraised for $290,000, the bank would only loan you $290,000. That means you would have to come up with the other $10,000 out of pocket. Be very careful paying more than the appraised value for a home. If prices start to decline, you could easily wind up owing more than the home is worth.

The last two things to consider when drafting an "offer they can't refuse", is setting the closing date and determining the amount of your earnest money deposit. When it comes to closing dates, the sooner the closing date the stronger the offer. Unless the seller requests additional time to relocate, the sooner you are able to close the deal and get them their money the better. Again, this is where removing contingencies and having a cash offer can make a big difference. A mortgage can take 30 to 45 days after your offer has been accepted to receive a clear to close. A cash offer could close in as little as 10 days. Keep this in mind when submitting your offer. I understand that having a cash offer may not be realistic, but do your best to keep your closing date under 45 days from offer acceptance. You can always ask for an extension if needed, but the seller may push back, so be prepared to negotiate.

The last thing to consider when drafting your offer is your earnest money deposit (EMD). An earnest money deposit is like a security deposit. It is the money you put down with your offer to show that you're a serious buyer. Once you close on the home, the earnest money goes towards your down payment. If you decide to back out of the purchase for a reason not outlined in one of your contingencies, you'll lose your earnest money deposit. The standard EMD is between 1% and 3% of the purchase price. If your offer is accepted, the EMD would be held in escrow until it is time to close on the purchase.

Remember, not all offers get accepted. It can be disappointing, but don't be discouraged. When submitting offers always make sure your price and terms are competitive and make sure you keep your

Seek & Destroy mentality. It may take several offers but if you stay persistent, eventually you will be successful.

Closing the deal – Once you get a house under contract, as a buyer it is up to you to close the deal. In most cases the first thing you will want to do is hire a professional inspector to inspect the home. A good agent should be able to recommend a home inspector. You can also search online, but make sure to read reviews and compare pricing. The inspection should be scheduled as soon as possible, especially if you have an inspection contingency. Most inspection contingencies have a deadline. This means if you do not respond by the deadline, you will no longer be able to get out of the contract without forfeiting your deposit. If you do run into scheduling issues, make sure you request an extension in writing. I would also recommend you be there for the inspection. It will help you get familiar with the home and if there are any issues you will be able to see them firsthand. Once the inspection is complete, the inspector should provide you with a detailed inspection report. If there are no major issues and you are comfortable with the condition of the home, you would notify the seller and proceed with purchase. If you do discover major issues or aren't comfortable with the condition of the home, you have two options. The first and most obvious option would be to walk away from the deal and exercise your "inspection contingency". The other option you have would be to try and negotiate with the seller. In most cases you would request one of three things. One you could ask the seller to repair the issue. A lot of sellers don't like this option because they don't want to spend any money and they don't want to be responsible for the repairs if they aren't done correctly. If the seller does agree to make the repair, make sure it is done professionally and be sure to inspect the repair before close. The second and more popular option would be to ask the seller for a credit at closing. This would allow you to make the repair on your own and exclude the seller from any responsibility regarding the repair. It will also save the seller from having to spend any money and lower the amount you have to bring to the closing table. Make sure you check with your lender before negotiating a closing credit. In some cases, closing credits are capped at a certain percentage. This means if major repairs are needed the credit may not be enough to cover the cost. In that case you may want to consider a third option. Similar to a seller credit, the third option would be to ask for a reduction in the sale price. A price reduction would also exclude the seller from any responsibility regarding the repair and save the seller from having to spend any money. There is also no limit on the size of a price reduction in the case a large repair is needed. Remember, this is your last chance to object to the condition of the property. After you release the inspection contingency you are saying you will accept the property as is.

The next step will be the appraisal. If you have given the property the L.I.A.R test, you know that after inspection (I) comes appraisal (A). However, this time the appraisal won't be done by you, it will be done by a professional appraiser selected by the bank. This appraisal will be used to determine the value of your home for the purpose of approving your mortgage.

The lender will select the appraiser, and you should work with the seller to schedule the appraisal. The appraiser will be looking at the condition and features of the home. They will also pull recent sales of comparable homes. After the appraisal is complete, the appraiser will issue an appraisal report. The appraisal report will list the details of the home, the comparable homes that were used, and the appraised fair market value. If the appraised value is higher or matches your offer price, you would satisfy any appraisal contingency. If the appraised value is lower than your offer price, you would need to make up the difference between the appraised value and the offer price. This can be done by coming up with the difference in cash or trying to re-negotiate with the seller to lower the price. You could also contest the appraisal and try to request a new one. Unfortunately, you may have to pay for the additional appraisal so make sure you have documentation to support your objection.

The final step to complete in the mortgage

process is called underwriting. Underwriting is basically the process of approving your mortgage. Some parts of the underwriting process begin when you are first pre-approved for a mortgage. For example, a credit check and income verification would be done during pre-approval. However, during underwriting, the bank will do a complete examination of your financial position. This would include investments, savings, retirement accounts, and employment history. They will also verify your identity and address history. With that said, during the underwriting process it is very important to have your documentation and records together so you can respond to requests quickly. For example, if the lender asks for your W2s or bank statements, you want to have these ready so can send them quickly and avoid a delay in your closing. Once you've met all the underwriters' requests and requirements, you will receive a "clear to close". A "clear to close" means that the lender has approved your mortgage and you can proceed to closing.

Closing day can be a stressful but exciting day. Before closing you should schedule a final walkthrough. I would recommend scheduling the morning of closing or as close to closing as possible. The purposer of your final walk through is to ensure the property is in the same condition as when you made your offer. You may also want to confirm any agreed-upon repairs are completed and the seller has moved out and removed any personal property that will not convey with the property. Once your final inspection is complete, it's time for the actual closing. You can expect to spend a few hours at the title company signing paperwork. Most title companies will provide you a list of any items to bring to closing. Once the signing is complete, you'll receive your keys and it's time to move in.

FLIPPING HOUSES

If you watch TV or have any interest in real estate investing, I'm sure you have heard the term "flipping houses". Flipping houses is when you buy a run down or outdated property, fix it up, and sell it for a profit. Flipping houses can be a great way to make money in real estate. However, it is not always as easy as it seems on HGTV. To be successful at flipping houses you must master the techniques discussed earlier in this chapter. That includes being able to give a potential real estate investment a lie detector or L.I.A.R test. You will also have to be an expert at "Seek & Destroy" and "closing the deal". Remember finding a house to flip is different than finding one to live in. Although some of the core principles are the same, you may have to develop different strategies to be successful. With that said, let's look at some key points to focus on when evaluating a fix-and-flip opportunity.

After Repair Value (ARV) - The after repair value

(ARV) is the value of the property after you fix it up. The ARV is very important in deciding whether or not a fix-and-flip opportunity will be successful. For example, say you find a property that is listed for $100,000 and it will cost you $25,000 to fix it up. That means your total investment would be roughly $125,000. If the after repair value of the property was $120,000, you could potentially lose $5000. On the other hand, if the after repair value was $150,000, you could potentially make $25,000. Now these are just rough estimates, but the idea is to show the importance of the ARV. Paying too much for a property or spending too much for repairs is the most common mistake investors make when executing a fix and flip. By calculating the ARV, you will have an idea of what you should be paying for the property and repairs. Use the tips outlined in the lie detector or L.I.A.R test to come up with an appraisal or ARV for the property. The only difference is you would consider the after-repair condition of the property. Once you have the ARV, you can use some simple calculations to determine a good price to pay for the property and repairs.

The 70% rule - The 70% rule says that you shouldn't pay more than 70% of the after repair value of a property minus the cost to fix it up. In our earlier example we had a property listed for $100,000 and a cost of $25,000 to fix it up. Using the after repair value of $150,000 lets apply the 70% rule. First take 70% of the ARV ($150,000 x 70% =$105,000). Next take 70% of the ARV and subtract the cost to fix it up ($105,000 - $25,000 = $80,000). In this example the most you would want to pay for this property is $80,000. Again, these are only rough estimates, but applying the 70% rule can help when comparing fix-and-flip opportunities.

Fix or Flop – I'm sure we have all seen the fix-and-flip shows on TV. The story is always the same. They buy the property and start fixing it up, when all of sudden they discover an issue they didn't plan for. Well, this doesn't just happen on TV. That is why one of the most important parts of a fix-and-flip is properly estimating the repair costs. A good investor must have a vision for every project and be able to execute that vison within budget. Before you begin calculating repair costs, understand what the vision will be for the project. Again, you can start with the lie detector or L.I.A.R test. Look at where the property is located. Is it a high–end neighborhood or does it have more moderately priced properties. In a moderately priced neighborhood, buyers may not want to pay more because you put in top-of-the-line appliances. If you're not familiar with the neighborhood, try to research some recently renovated comps or look for an open house of a similar home. Remember your vision must match your budget and your budget must match your vision. Over or under improving a property is a common mistake and can quickly affect your profits at the closing table.

Once you have a vision for your project, the next step is to inspect the property. When inspecting a fix-and-flip opportunity, the first thing to check for is big ticket items. That includes things like a roof, foundation, mold, and HVAC. Big ticket items can quickly deplete a renovation budget, especially if the repairs are unexpected. Make sure to be thorough when inspecting the property. I would recommend going room by room and write down any needed repairs. For example, does the room need paint or flooring? Does it need new light and door fixtures? Write down as many notes as possible and try to include quantities and size for each room. Also make sure to take a lot of pictures. Even the most detailed person can miss something. Having lots of pictures and videos will you help you later on when you are trying to put together your renovation budget.

Now that you've completed the inspection of the property, it's time to calculate your renovation budget. For some investors this step may be completed by a contractor. However, if you are still in the evaluation stage, you may want to create an estimated repair budget to see if the property could be potentially profitable. Remember, estimating repair costs takes experience. As a beginner you should first focus on material cost. Start by listing out each room of the property. Then list out all the material that will be needed to renovate that space. Try to be as detailed as possible. For example, renovating a bathroom may require a vanity, toilet, sink fixtures, shower fixtures, tile for shower, tile for floor, and light fixtures. Once you have listed out as much material as possible, it's time to head over to your local Home Depot or Lowes. You can also go online, but if you are new to renovations, I would recommend visiting the store, so you get a better feel for the quality of the material. That $29.00 light fixture might look great online, but when you see it in person it might look more like a night light. Again, estimating repair costs takes experience. As you begin to gain experience you will not need to put as much effort into this part of the process. Once you become more familiar with brands and costs, you will be able to reuse prior estimates to quickly come up with a repair budget. You can also reuse a repair estimate from a contractor to quickly gauge rehab costs. The goal is to be as accurate as possible and when in doubt overestimate. It is always better to end up with a surprise savings than a surprise expense.

Time is money – As I stated earlier, if you decide to pursue house flipping, you must become an expert at "Seek & Destroy" and "closing the deal". For that reason, we are not going to revisit these topics. But if you need a refresher, you can reference these sections under "Buying a home". For this section we are going to assume you have got your property under contract and closed the deal. With that said, this is where the clock starts, and the real work begins. Remember time is money. The goal of any fix and flip is to buy, repair, and resale the property as quick as possible. The longer it takes for you to repair and get the home sold, the more your costs will increase. This means you must have a plan. If you are doing some of the work yourself, be prepared to dedicate the next couple months of your life to the project. Only working on the project in the evenings and on weekends isn't going to be enough and will cost you money. If you are using contractors make sure you manage your expectations and communicate with them frequently. I would also recommend having back up contractors available in case a change is needed mid project. That's why it is important to get multiple bids from multiple contractors. Try to be in and out in less than six weeks. This means from the day of closing to the day you put the home back on the market should be roughly 45 days.

Once you have completed your repairs, it's time to get the home ready for sale. First thing is to do a full inspection of the property. Make sure there is no unfinished details or construction debris. You may want to consider having someone professionally clean the house. You want buyers to be excited about the home and there is never a second chance to make a first impression. You will also want to consider staging the property. Staged properties sell faster and for more money. However, a staging company may charge between $1,000 and $4,000 to stage a property. You can also consider virtual staging if that's not in the budget. Work with your agent to formulate a marketing plan that works for you. An open house soon after the property is listed is always a good idea.

Remember flipping houses is challenging and no investment is guaranteed. Always have a plan and try your best to stick to it. I would recommend starting with a smaller project until you gain experience. Your first project will not be easy, however if you take the time to do your research and put in the work, it can be a great investment opportunity.

AIRBNB

By now I'm sure everyone is familiar with Airbnb. For those who are not familiar, Airbnb is an online platform that allows property owners to list their homes for short term rental. Whether it is their entire home, a basement apartment, or a spare bedroom, Airbnb has become a popular way for people to make money with the homes they live in or other properties they own. Once you have decided to be a host on Airbnb there are several things to consider before getting started.

What to consider before starting Airbnb

What is your goal? - Yes, we all want to make some money but what is your goal? Are you just trying to make some extra income? Or are you trying to build a short term rental empire? Depending on your goals, the amount of time and money involved will be different. So first determine what type of host you want to be. I recommend starting small

Know the rules – Like we discussed in earlier chapters, whenever evaluating a real estate opportunity you should always give a property a L.I.A.R test. Airbnb and short term rental opportunities are no different. Especially when it comes to the last part; "Rules". The laws surrounding Airbnb and short term rentals vary from city to city and are constantly changing. Many of these rules place limits on how many days a property can be rented. They also may place restrictions on the types of properties that can be rented. For example, an owner-occupied property may be allowed to rent 180 days a year, where as an investment property may not be eligible for Airbnb and short term rental. So bottom-line make sure you know the rules in your area.

Time is money - Managing a successful Airbnb listing takes time and money. Make sure you have the time to invest, especially in the beginning. This includes investing time and money to stage and photograph the property. A properly staged listing and great photographs can be the difference between a successful listing and an unsuccessful one. Once the property has been staged and listed, you must ensure the property is adequately maintained. This of course means routine cleaning and restocking of any essentials. You will also be responsible for responding to any emergencies. All of this will take time and or money and sometimes much more than you expected. So, make sure you have the time and energy to do what is necessary.

Nosey neighbors - Whether you own or rent, most of us have neighbors. Some neighbors can be like family, but some can be your worst enemy. So, make sure you consider what type of neighbors you have when considering listing a property for Airbnb. Since the inception of Airbnb, there has been plenty of controversy regarding Airbnb especially in residential neighborhoods. If you live in one of these neighborhoods or have "nosey neighbors", you'll want to be extra careful before listing on Airbnb. Decide if the potential headaches that come from nosey neighbors are worth the effort to host on Airbnb.

Risk & liability - When you are hosting on Airbnb, you are literally inviting complete strangers into your home. If the idea of that alone makes you feel uneasy, you'll need to think long and hard about hosting on Airbnb. If having strangers staying with you is not an option, your only Airbnb route is to find and acquire a dedicated rental unit. Outside of personal safety, you are exposing yourself to a host of other risks by hosting on Airbnb. You're putting your property at risk for theft and damage. You could also be at risk of renting to a squatter. Not to mention the potential liability if your guests get injured or cause damage to other properties like your neighbors. With that said, Airnb does offer $1 million in liability insurance coverage to minimize much of these risks

So, after taking the above into consideration, do you still want to start an Airbnb? If so, you will need to make a plan. Below is 6-point checklist to get you started and help take your Airbnb from an idea to business. Now this assumes you already have property secured. If not start with the chapter on real estate and come back once you have secured a property.

Airbnb 6-point Checklist

1. Start an account – I know that seems simple, but you would be surprised how many questions will be answered just by signing up for an account. In most cases the app will help walk you through the listing process.

2. Clean and stage – This could be as simple as sprucing up a guest bedroom, or as extensive as doing a full renovation. Either way you will want to make sure the space is clean, stylish, and functional.

3. A picture is worth 1000 words – This will be the most important part of your listing. Especially in the beginning before renters have had the opportunity to post reviews. With that said, make sure your pictures exaggerate the best features of your space and minimize any potential negatives. Now I'm not saying to "catfish" prospective renters, but highlight the good. For example, if your property has a pool, gourmet kitchen, or even a king-size bed, be sure to capture a photo of these features in their best possible condition. As for negatives, if the space is small, try to take a wide-angle photo. You can also highlight its functionality. Like maybe an espresso maker, big screen T.V., or great storage. Whatever the case, make sure you invest the time or money into getting great photos.

4. Talk is cheap – A good description of the property always helps, but remember talk is cheap. Stay away from talking up your property with words like "luxurious", or "lavish". What's luxury to one person may be basic to another. Plus, your pictures should exemplify the taste level of the space. When writing your description try to stick to the facts. If you are in a great location, make sure to mention that. One block from the beach will stand out way more than "luxurious" studio apartment. Use the description to also answer any logistical questions. Is the property close to public transportation or is there parking available? The more questions you can answer for a potential renter, the greater the chance they will want to book and the less questions you will have to respond to.

5. Figure out entry and exit – You must have an access and security plan for Airbnb. Even if that means you check in and check out each guest yourself. That method is probably not the best option, and I would highly recommend you automate the process. You can find keyless entry locks at Home Depot or Lowes. This will allow you to provide the guest a passcode for entry and exit. This code can also be changed after each stay to ensure it is not used more than once. I would also recommend investing in a wireless camera. Even if it's just a ring camera on the front door. This way you can monitor the property without having to physically be there. As your bookings increase, having the option to automate entry will be priceless.

6. Cleaning and maintenance – Just like entry and exit, a cleaning and maintenance plan is essential to a successful Airbnb. Again, to start that could mean you clean the space after each stay. However, as your bookings increase, this could be more and more time consuming. Eventually you may want to hire someone to take care of cleaning. The good thing is Airbnb allows you to add a cleaning fee to cover some of the expense.

CHAPTER SIX: CARS

For most people a car is their first major purchase. It may also be the first time they get introduced to credit and use a loan to make a purchase. Unfortunately, it can also be one of their first financial mistakes. In this chapter we are going to go over the things to consider when buying a car. Especially if you plan on financing the car and maintaining a car payment. Remember, a car is an asset that in most cases depreciates with time. That means unlike a house, over time a car will be worth less than what you paid for it. With that said, my biggest advice is to look at a car as simply a form of transportation. Eventually that new car smell will be gone, and those tires will need to be changed. However, that car payment will be the same. There is nothing worse than making payments on a car that's broken down, needs repair, or you no longer like because it has lost its excitement to drive.

5 THINGS TO CONSIDER WHEN BUYING A CAR

1. Lifestyle – People buy cars for a number of reasons. Some buy simply for transportation, while others buy for pleasure or status. Regardless of why you are buying, it is important to consider your lifestyle when selecting a vehicle. So first look under your own roof. Are you single? Do you have a wife and kids? That new corvette might look great, but trust me there won't be much room for car seats. You should also consider the location you are in. Does it snow? Do you have a long commute to work? All these things are important when considering a car purchase. Especially if this will be your primary or only vehicle. There is nothing worse than having a car that no longer fits your lifestyle, and chances are you will be looking to trade it in when it doesn't.

2. New or used – The second thing to consider is should you buy a new or used vehicle. My personal preference is to always buy used. That is because buying a used car is typically the least expensive option and you tend to get more car for your money. You also avoid a large portion of the depreciation that come with new cars. Remember a car is an asset that depreciates with time and cars lose the most value in the first year. That means that a hundred-thousand-dollar car will only be worth 50k in about 5 years. Think about it. A new car is only new until the next year's model comes out. Unless you plan on buying a new car every year, you will always be chasing the latest model. Ask yourself is it worth paying up to 30% more for a car that may be outdated in a few months. With that said, used cars aren't for everyone, and as of late used car prices have been increasing. If your main concern is the warranty that comes with a new car, I would recommend looking at a certified vehicle. These days certified vehicles come with great warranties and are still priced far cheaper than buying new.

Regardless of what you decide, make sure to consider which option is best for you. Knowing whether you want a new or used vehicle will help with your search and finding the best deal for the car and financing. Lenders tend to offer better rates on new vehicles. However, it may not be enough to outweigh the premium in price.

3. Run the numbers – Buying a car can be a lot like buying a home. It's all about the numbers. Your credit score, income, debt to income ratio, and your down payment are all numbers you need to know when considering a car purchase. So, make sure you know this information and run the numbers BEFORE you go to the dealership. Once you get an idea of the type of vehicle you want and its price, I would recommend using a payment calculator to get an estimate of the monthly payment. You should be able to make this monthly payment comfortably. A common guideline people use is the 20/4/10 rule. The 20/4/10 rule says with a 20% down payment on a four-year car loan you should spend no more than 10% of your monthly income. Again, this is just a guideline and might not work for everyone. However, I would recommend finding a less expensive vehicle before taking on a high car note. Trust me the dealership will have no problem signing you up, but will be ghost when you can't make the payment.

4. License, insurance, & registration – Every driver needs a license, and every vehicle requires insurance and registration. Anyone that has ever been pulled over knows the first thing a police officer asks for is "license, insurance, and registration". With that said, please consider these 3 things before buying a car. I know you are saying to yourself "that's obvious", but you would be surprised how many people take this for granted. I know people who have bought cars with no drivers license and we all know people who have driven cars with expired insurance or registration. I strongly recommend not doing this. It's not worth the trouble and can become a very expensive mistake. Be sure to consider insurance and registration costs in your monthly car budget. Also do your best to address any tickets or violations as soon as possible. These issues tend to get worse and more expensive the longer it takes to resolve. Believe me, you don't want to be making car payments on a car that can't be driven (legally).

5. Maintenance, parking, and security - Last but not least you must consider maintenance, parking, and security before buying a vehicle. These three things are often overlooked, but are some of the most common expenses that come with owning a car. The most important and probably the most expensive is maintenance. Regular car maintenance will help to extend the life of your vehicle and will ultimately help it maintain its value. With that said, you may be able to delay certain car maintenance, but skipping it completely will cost you in the long run. Understand that some vehicles are more expensive to maintain than others. I learned this the hard way after purchasing a used 2000 Range Rover 4.6. If you ever heard the Jay-Z song "Imaginary Player", there is a famous line that says "what's the difference between a 4.0 and a 4.6? Like 30 to 40 grand". Let's just say the maintenance might also cost 30 to 40 grand. By the end of it, I probably spent more for repairs and maintenance than I did for the truck itself. That's why I would recommend researching the maintenance costs associated with certain vehicles. Especially if you are considering buying a foreign vehicle like Mercedes, BMW, Audi, or Land Rover. You do not want to be making payments on a car that doesn't run and you can't afford to fix. Trust me I know. And before I forget, I must mention one of the biggest maintenance expenses and that's gas. Different vehicles take different types and use different amounts of gas. These days a large SUV may take $100 just to fill up and if you are driving it every day that might not last you a week. Most foreign vehicles like Mercedes or BMWs require premium gasoline which can cost as much as $1 more per gallon. It might not sound like a lot, but it can add up quick, especially when gas prices spike to almost $5 per gallon. So, keep that in mind when you are deciding on your next vehicle. It may be worth considering an

EV.

Next you have parking & security. Now these expenses will depend heavily on your lifestyle. And when I say lifestyle, I mean mainly where you live and where you work. If you live and work in a rural area, parking may not be a big issue or expense. However, if you live or work in a larger city, you could expect to pay $100s of dollars per month for parking. It is not uncommon for apartments in the city to charge over $300 per month for an assigned parking space. Assigned parking in an office building could cost about the same. You can see how monthly parking expenses can add up quickly and who wants to be paying more for parking than they do for the car itself. Regardless, make sure you consider your parking options when deciding to buy a car. Parking your car in the wrong place or not having the correct "parking pass" can lead to your car getting towed. Trust me getting your car towed is one of the worst car ownership experiences there is. Not to mention getting your car back is not cheap. And we can't talk about parking without mentioning parking tickets. Every car owner I know has had them and they can be a real headache. My advice is to always pay the meter, only park where its legal, and if you get a ticket pay it. Parking ticket fines normally double after a couple weeks, and too many unpaid tickets can lead to your car getting booted and or towed.

The last thing to consider is security. Now depending on your parking options, the security of your vehicle may not be an issue. For example, if you park your vehicle in a garage at your home, chances are your vehicle will be safe. However, parking in the lot at your apartment complex might make your vehicle an easy target. The bottom-line is no matter where you park, if you have something a thief wants, they are going to do their best to steal it. So, your job is to take steps to stop them or at least deter them. Some steps you can take are getting an alarm, installing wheel locks on your rims, and never keep any valuables in your car. You should also research what cars are most vulnerable. Thieves like to target specific cars. Recently it was discovered that Kia's and Hyundai's were being stolen using a USB cord causing thefts of these vehicles to spike upwards of 800% in some areas. All because the vehicles did not have sufficient security features. So, before you go buy that Hyundai, Kia, or even that Dodge Hell Cat, understand it could make you a target. Replacing a set of tires and rims could be thousands of dollars and even worse being carjacked could cost you your life. Keep this in mind when selecting a vehicle, and always have a plan to protect it.

BUYING A CAR

Buying a car can be a challenge. Especially if you plan on purchasing from a dealer. Car salesman don't always have the best reputation and as buyer you always want to get the best deal. In this section will discuss some important steps to take once you have decided to purchase a vehicle. We will also discuss tips for negotiating with car salesman. For most people a car is a major purchase and one you will have to live with for several years. Following these tips will ensure you buy with confidence and help to avoid buyer's remorse.

DO YOUR RESEARCH

In today's car market the most important thing you can do when buying a car is to research. The internet has changed the car market and made it easier to find the car you want at the best price. However, before you can begin your research, we recommend you review the "5 Things to Consider When Buying a Car" discussed earlier in this chapter. This will help you narrow down your list of prospective vehicles. Remember it's a waste of time to research sports cars when you really need an SUV, and don't get your hopes up searching for BMWs when you can only afford a Nissan. Once you've settled on a few car candidates, it's time to start your research.

The first thing you can do is go to a site like www.cargurus.com or www.autotrader.com. Next enter the make and model of the cars you are interested in and get an idea of what they are selling for. Once you have the estimated cost, it is time to run the numbers. You can use the 20/4/10 rule to get an idea of how much the car will cost you and its affordability. Most sites also have payment calculators that will help you run the numbers and get an estimated monthly payment. Don't forget to consider insurance and parking as a part of your monthly expenses. After you have found a vehicle that fits your needs and that you can comfortably afford, it's time to research the cars' reliability. This could be as simple as googling the cars make and model followed by the word "reliability". The internet is full of car reviews and it should be easy to find one for the vehicle you are interested in. You should look for any glaring issues, like recalls or a large volume of customer complaints. Now would also be the time to investigate the maintenance costs associated with the vehicle. I also recommend researching how close the nearest dealership is to you. All maintenance doesn't have to be done at the dealership, but certain recalls may require the work be done by a dealer. If the nearest dealership is far from where you live or in a completely different city, it could become difficult to get the vehicle fixed. I remember having to have the Range Rover I mentioned earlier, towed to a city an hour away because that was the closest dealership and the only place that could do the work. Always keep this in mind when researching a vehicle for purchase.

At this point you should have a short list of potential vehicles. So, if you haven't already, it's time to see them in person. Yes, that means it's time to window shop. Be careful because depending on where you go, you might run into a salesperson trying to pressure you to buy. That's why I recommend going somewhere like CarMax. They have no haggle pricing, so it is more of a no pressure environment. They also carry a wide range of vehicles for you to explore and compare. With that said, if you can't get to a CarMax and must go to a local dealer, just make sure you are clear that you are only looking and not ready to buy today. Once you find a car you are interested in, make sure you check it out thoroughly. Sit in it and if you have someone with you have them sit behind you. When my wife and I go car shopping, we bring the car seats to see how they will fit in the new vehicle. You would be surprised how many vehicles look big until you get in them. If after your initial review, the car still meets your needs, it's time to drive it. Try to get to a highway or somewhere you can at least get to 60 mph. Pay attention to the acceleration, handling, steering, and braking. Also drive with the radio off and windows down to listen for any noises or issues. Once you get back to the lot test out all the features like the radio, navigation, heating and cooling. If the car performs well, the next step is to give the keys back to the dealer and leave. It is not time to buy. Go through this process with at least 3 vehicles. Compare the pros and cons of each and give yourself some time to decide. Remember buying a car is a big decision, so don't rush into it. Doing the proper research will ensure you buy with confidence.

NEGOTIATING & CAR SALESMAN

They say the price is what you pay, and the value is what you get. When buying a car, the goal is to make sure the price is never greater than the value. Unfortunately, this can be harder than you think and may take some negotiating. With that said, the car market has changed significantly over the past decade. Dealers like CarMax and Carvana offer no-haggle or value pricing, which means the price is non-negotiable. For some this makes for a simpler and less stressful car buying experience. In fact, as the car market has become more competitive due to inventory shortages, you may find even traditional dealers are less likely to negotiate price. However, if you decide to try your hand at negotiating there are certain rules you must follow. Remember car salesman are professionals and the only way to get a good deal is by earning it. Below we will go over 10 tips for negotiating with car salesman. By following these tips, you will increase your chances of getting a great deal on a vehicle.

10 TIPS FOR CAR NEGOTIATIONS

1. Control your emotions – Buying a car can be an exciting experience. It can also be tiring and stressful. Car salesmen understand this and will use all these emotions against you in negotiations. It's not uncommon for them to keep you waiting in the dealership for hours in hopes that you will become exhausted and accept whatever it is their offering. The goal here is to control your emotions. Be patient and stay focused. Also make sure you eat something before you go. There is nothing worse than becoming "hangry" during car negotiations. Also don't be afraid to leave or take a break if you are not comfortable. It is always better to walk away than accept a bad deal.

2. Say less – Everything you say will be used against you when buying a car. I know that sounds like you're under arrest, but in car negotiations remember you have the right to remain silent. Don't start talking about how bad you need a new car or how much you love the vehicle you are looking at. Try to avoid the small talk and try to ask more questions than you answer. A dealer's job is to size you up, so answering questions about down payments, credit scores, or trade ins, will give them the upper hand in negotiations. With that said, save those conversations until you have found the vehicle you want and are ready to negotiate the price. It is ok to say "I don't know" or decline to give them your financial information early in the process.

3. Don't go alone – Car salesmen have a whole team working to sell you a car. So if you go to a dealership by yourself, you may feel out numbered. That is why I recommend bringing someone with you. It always helps to have a second opinion when making decisions. It can also help with negotiations. Have you ever heard of good cop/bad cop. If you haven't, good cop/bad cop is a psychological tactic used in negotiations. The good cop would take a positive or more friendly position, and the bad cop would take a negative or more aggressive position. If done correctly it can force the car salesman to work harder because instead of having to convince one person, they need to convince two. With that said, I must warn you about bringing someone with you. Make sure it is someone you trust and who's opinion you respect. You don't want to bring someone who might influence you to accept a bad deal.

4. Avoid credit checks – One of the first questions a car salesman will ask is if you will be financing your vehicle purchase. If you say yes, the next request will be for them to check your credit. Your response should be "no thank you". First, before you step on the lot you should already know what your score is and what kind of interest rate you qualify for. Second, dealerships make money when you use their financing. Letting them pull your credit can affect the type of deal you get and what you pay for the car. Also, a hard credit pull can negatively affect your credit score. With that said, resist early requests to run your credit, and only do a credit application when you are sure you want to buy the car.

5. Negotiate price not payment – Another popular question dealers ask is "how much can you afford each month?". Do not fall for this trick and keep your answer to yourself. Dealers often use the monthly payment to divert your attention away from the total cost of the vehicle. Monthly payments can easily be lowered by extending the length of the loan. Unfortunately, the longer the loan the more it will cost you in interest. That is why we recommend negotiating the price not the payment. Remember, do your research before you step on the lot. You should already have an idea of how much vehicle you can afford and what the monthly payment will be. Use this to your advantage and focus on lowering the price of the vehicle not the monthly payment.

6. Save your trade-in – In today's market, used cars and trade-ins are becoming more and more valuable. For this reason, dealerships are focusing on trade-ins as a source of profit. With that said, don't be surprised if you are asked about your trade in very early in the process. If you plan on trading in a vehicle, I recommend holding off on any trade-in talk until you have found a vehicle of interest and have begun negotiating the price. And again, do your research. You should know how much your car is worth and what you owe on the car before stepping on the lot. To get the value of the car you can start by checking Kelly Blue Book. However, if you want to get a true value, and one you can use in negotiations, I recommend going to CarMax. CarMax will do an inspection of your vehicle and give you a written offer good for 7 days. Most dealerships are willing to beat this offer and at worst match it. Either way, it will give you a solid price to start negotiations for your trade-in.

7. Avoid the extras – Car dealerships don't make money off cars; they make money off everything else. That means they make money when you use their financing or purchase the warranties, insurance, service packages, and a host of other extras they will try to sell you. My advice is to avoid the extras. It will only increase the cost of the vehicle and statistics say they are not worth it. If you do decide to get a warranty, insurance, or other add on, see if they can include it free of charge or at least discount it.

8. Know your financing – It is important to know your financial position. We touched on this earlier when we discussed credit checks. Before you step on the lot, you should already know what your score is and what kind of interest rate you qualify for. Car dealerships make money when you use their financing. To ensure you get the best deal, I recommend getting pre-qualified. That way you will know if the rate they are offering is competitive. Most dealerships will do their best to match or beat your interest rate.

9. Timing – Timing makes a difference in vehicle negotiations. Car dealerships have yearly, quarterly and monthly sales quotas. That means at the end of month or end of the year, dealers are more willing to make deals and cut prices. Keep this in mind when you are planning to make a purchase. If you can wait, look to make your purchase in October, November, or December. If you can't wait until the end of the year, look to purchase during the last week of the month. Holidays like Black Friday, New Years' Eve, and President's Day are also good times to find deals on cars. Also try to avoid weekends. Early in the week and mornings are good times. It will be less crowded and allow you to have the salesperson's full attention.

10. Be prepared to walk away – This is simple. Don't feel obligated or pressured to make a deal. If you are not sure about the purchase, get up and leave. Take a day or two to think it over. Remember, it is better to walk away than make a purchase you will regret later. Plus, it will let the salesperson know you are firm in what you are willing to pay. I've had dealers call me after leaving offering to accept the price they were refusing before. Understand for the most part, cars are a depreciating asset. The longer a car sits on the lot, the less its worth and the more it costs the dealer. With that said, do your best to be patient and remember time is on your side.

CHAPTER SEVEN: INVESTMENTS

Warren Buffett once said, "Don't be proud of your salary be proud of your investments". That is because investing is the key to financial success. Through investing, you will be able to decrease the time spent working for money and spend that time letting your money work for you. To do this you must first understand what investing is. Put simply, investing is the process of buying an asset with the expectation it will increase in value. That could mean buying real-estate, stocks, crypto, or even a Rolex watch. Whatever the asset, if there is a market, and a return can be made it can be considered an investment. With that said, every investment is made up of three key characteristics. These characteristics include risk, return, and liquidity.

Risk - Risk is the probability your investment will produce a loss rather than a profit. It is also one of the first things to consider when evaluating an investment opportunity. In most cases, the greater the risk the greater the return and vice versa the lower the risk the lower the return. You must be comfortable with risk when deciding to invest. If you have a low risk tolerance, it may be better to find an investment that offers lower risk. You don't want to be losing sleep because you are worrying about your investments.

Return - The next thing to consider is the return. This is commonly called R.O.I. for return on investment. R.O.I. is simply the profit or money made on an investment. Analyzing ROI is a great way to compare potential investment opportunities that may come with similar risks. For example, say you had an opportunity that required an investment of $10,000 and had a potential return on investment of $1000. Next say you had an opportunity that required an investment of $50,000 and had a potential return on investment of $3000. On the surface it may appear the second opportunity with a return of $3000 would be a better investment. However, the second investment would require 5 times the investment for only 3 times the return. That said, the first investment would have a higher return. A simple formula for calculating R.O.I. is return divided by investment. In the examples above, the first investment would have a R.O.I. of 10 % ($1000/$10,000) and the second investment would have an R.O.I of 6% ($3000/$50,000). Again, you can use this formula to quickly compare potential investment opportunities that have similar risk.

Liquidity - Finally, you should always look at the liquidity of an investment. Liquidity is the ability to sell or "liquidate" an investment. Like risk, the liquidity of an investment will have a direct affect on its potential return. That said, you can expect to receive a higher return for an investment with low liquidity. Whereas, a highly liquid investment may have a potentially lower return. To give you an example, a house or other forms of real estate would not be considered liquid. That is because it could take months to sell and finally receive cash for your investment. A rare painting would also have low liquidity. Precious objects and collectables often have a limited or select number of buyers, which make selling more difficult. Again, the harder to sell the lower the liquidity. On the other hand, investments like stocks, bonds, and some crypto currencies would be considered highly liquid investments. That is because they can be converted to cash relatively quickly. If you have ever bought and sold stock using an app like Robinhood, you know a stock can be liquidated or sold in a matter of seconds. That is why liquidity is so important when it comes to investments. If the value of your investment begins to drop quickly, being able to sell and cut your losses becomes increasingly important. The higher the liquidity, the easier it will be to sell. This is also important in the case you have an emergency, or another investment opportunity presents itself. Having the ability to quickly liquidate an investment will give you the flexibility to adapt and restructure your investment portfolio.

Investment strategy – Before you begin on your investment journey, it is important to create a basic investment strategy. The first step in creating an investment strategy is to look at your current financial situation. You will want to look at your monthly income and expenses to help determine how much you will have to invest. You will also want to look at any outstanding debts or liabilities that may affect your ability to invest. Remember, it doesn't take a lot of money to begin investing, and it is better to invest a little than to not invest at all. Next you should decide on your investment approach. Mainly do you want to be an active investor or a passive investor. Active investing is more of a hands-on approach while passive investing is more of a buy and hold strategy. For example, day trading stock options or buying houses to fix and flip would be considered an active investment approach. While investing in index funds or buying a rental property would be considered more of a passive investment approach. Both can be successful, however passive investing presents less risk and may be better suited for people just starting out. Lastly you will want to consider your goals. Are you investing for retirement or looking for an immediate return? Knowing this will be important when deciding what type of investments to pursue. With so many different investment options, an investment strategy will help you decide which opportunities are right for you. That said, let's look at five common types of investments.

5 TYPES OF INVESTMENTS

1. Stocks & EFTs – Stocks or equity securities are financial assets that represent ownership in a company. Corporations issue stock in the form of shares as a way to raise funds and grow a company. Public companies list their stock on exchanges, like the Nasdaq or the New York Stock Exchange (NYSE). Buyers and sellers then use stockbrokers to purchase and sell stock from these exchanges. By purchasing shares of a company's stock, you would obtain an ownership interest in that company and be what is called a shareholder. Shareholders have voting rights, are entitled to dividends, and have the right to sell the shares they own. That said, there are two main ways to earn income from stocks. Those are dividends and appreciation. Dividends are a distribution of company's profits in the form of cash payments. They are paid on a per share basis and the amount is determined by the company's board of directors. The other way to earn money from stocks is through capital appreciation. Appreciation is simply an increase in the share price or value of the stock. For example, if you bought a share for $100 and it is now worth $150 you would have gained $50 through appreciation of the stock. Over time, appreciation offers investors the greatest potential for profit. At the same time, there are no guarantees when it comes to stocks and the stock market. Poor company performance, volatile market conditions, and a bad economy can all have a negative impact on a stocks share price. For this reason, stocks are generally considered a high-risk investment. However, using a buy-and-hold strategy can help to mitigate the risk of stock investment. That is because historically stocks outperform other investment classes when held over a long period of time.

    Another investment option similar to stocks are ETFs. ETF stands for Exchange-traded fund. Like stocks, ETFs are listed on the New York Stock Exchange

(NYSE) and can be purchased in shares. The main difference between stocks and ETFs is stocks represent a share of one individual company, while ETFs can be made up of hundreds or thousands of companies. The fact that ETFs can be made up of companies from various industries or sectors, make them popular with investors seeking diversification. Diversification can help reduce the risk of a downward swing in a single stock. However, that also means you won't benefit as much from a large upward swing in a single stock. Simply put, an ETF offers increased stability when compared to individual stocks. This makes it an attractive investment if you are looking for steadily increasing earnings over the long term.

2. CDs & Bonds – CDs and bonds are some of the safest investments you can make. Both offer returns with little to no risk and provide an alternative to a traditional savings account. A CD stands for certificate of deposit. A CD is a type of savings account that pays interest on a fixed lump sum deposit. In return, you agree not to withdraw your money during the term of the CD. The term of a CD can range from as short as six months, to as long as 5 years. In most cases, the longer the term, the higher the interest rate will be. However, if the principal deposit is withdrawn early or prior to the end of the term, you will most likely face a penalty that could eliminate most or all your interest earnings. For example, say you deposit $1,000 in a 12-month CD that has an annual percentage yield of 4%. During the 12-month term you would not be allowed to withdraw your money without facing a penalty. At the end of the first year, your CD would be worth $1,040 giving you a profit of $40. Now some may not consider this a true investment, since the return is much lower than other investment options. However, with low-risk comes low-reward and CDs are as safe as it gets. In fact, the Federal Deposit Insurance Corporation (FDIC) guarantees them up to $250,000.

  Bonds are another low-risk investment option. Like CDs, bonds pay interest on a fixed lump sum deposit. They also come with a time commitment and the possibility of penalty for early withdrawal. Bonds are normally issued by governments and companies looking to raise money. The bonds are then backed by the government or organization that issues them. This means, if that government or company fails, you could potentially lose your principal investment. For this reason, bonds are rated by agencies like Moody's and Standard & Poor's. The bond rating will assess the creditworthiness of the government or organization issuing the bond. The highest possible bond rating is AAA and U.S. Treasury bonds are the most common AAA rated bonds. Again, CDs and bonds are some of the safest investments that also have high liquidity. However, the returns can be modest and are geared for a more conservative investment strategy.

3. Cryptocurrency – Cryptocurrency or crypto for short is a relatively new investment class. Cryptocurrency is a digital currency or asset that began with the creation of the Bitcoin blockchain. Over the past four years, there has been an explosion of interest in crypto. That said, there has also been a growing concern regarding the stability and longevity of cryptocurrency. The collapse of the crypto exchange FTX and the drastic decline in prices has proven that crypto as an investment can be highly unpredictable. For this reason, cryptocurrency should be considered high risk and purely speculative. To begin investing in crypto, consider buying crypto directly, a crypto ETF, or "crypto stocks". Remember, it is important to manage risk with all investments but even more so with cryptocurrency. Make sure you have a plan, use a reputable crypto exchange, and only invest what you can afford to lose.

4. Real estate – Real estate is one of the oldest and most reliable investment options in history. Business tycoon Andrew Carnegie once said, "Ninety percent of all millionaires become so through owning real estate". Real estate can include vacant land, residential properties, and commercial properties. That means any property you buy with the intention of making money can be considered real estate investing. This includes buying a home to live in, purchasing a rental or Airbnb, or acquiring a fix and flip. Real estate is widely considered to be a low-risk investment as real estate tends to appreciate overtime. However, it is important to note that real estate is not considered a highly liquid investment. In the case you need to sell your property quickly, you could be forced to sell below market or at a loss. For this reason, it is best to consider real estate as a longer-term investment. For more information on real-estate investing, make sure to read chapter 5 which covers real estate in detail.

5. Precious Object – Anything of value purchased with the goal of reselling for profit can be considered an investment. That is why precious objects should be considered investments. Precious objects include gold, silver, rare coins, and jewelry. It can also include artwork, comic books, sports memorabilia, and rare tennis shoes. The fact is, if its value appreciates overtime, someone will invest in it. That said, investing in precious objects, especially "collectables", can be highly volatile. Niche markets usually have fewer buyers and with fewer buyers comes low liquidity and higher risk. Precious objects are also prone to physical damage. Special attention must be given to how they are stored and maintained. Keep this in mind as the quality and condition of the object will play a big part in its value.

DO YOUR RESEARCH

Benjamin Franklin once said, "An investment in knowledge pays the best interest". Well, when it comes to making investments, this could not be more true. Whether it be stocks, real-estate, or comic books, it is important to do your research. In fact, before you invest in anything, I would recommend you learn as much information as possible. That means not only understanding the market or industry you are investing in, but also know the markets or industries that may impact your investment. You should also research any regulations or laws that can affect your investment. The more you know, the better your chances are of being successful. Understand that current and future trends are important, but the past also has a history of repeating itself. In the end, research could be the difference between a significant profit or a heart-breaking loss. Invest wisely and good luck.

CHAPTER EIGHT: STARTING YOUR OWN BUSINESS

Now more than ever the desire to be an entrepreneur and own your own business has grown tremendously. Since the start of the pandemic, applications for new businesses have gone up over 20 percent. The allure of being your own boss and the freedom and flexibility to make your own schedule has been a major motivation for people to try their hand at entrepreneurship. That said, starting a business can be challenging. Studies have shown that 50 percent of small businesses fail within the first 5 years. Whether due to lack of funds, poor planning, or simply bad timing, entrepreneurship has its risks. However, don't let this scare you away from entrepreneurship. Creating a successful business may take work, but with the proper plan it is achievable. Below are five things to consider before starting your own business. Use them as a guide as you begin on your journey to becoming an entrepreneur.

5 THINGS TO CONSIDER BEFORE STARTING YOUR OWN BUSINESS

1. Why do you want to start a business – This is the most important question to ask yourself. Why do you want to be a business owner? Is it the money, the freedom, your family, or some other reason? This will be important when deciding what type of business to start. For example, if you are in it for the money, you may want to stay away from businesses with low profit margins. Likewise, if you are looking to have more freedom you may not want to start a business that requires you to actively manage it. I would also recommend you find something you enjoy doing. Ask yourself what you would do if money wasn't an issue. Think about what motivates and inspires you. Having passion for what you are doing will greatly improve your chances of creating a successful business.

2. Will it be full-time or a side hustle – These days everyone seems to have a side hustle. A side hustle is a great way to make extra money outside of your full-time job. The other great thing about a side hustle is they often turn into full-time businesses. Regardless, whether you are starting a side hustle or a full-time venture, it is important to know the difference. That said, a side hustle typically demands less of your time. Side hustles also tend to generate immediate profits but have less potential for growth. On the other hand, a full-time venture will require a lot more of your time. It may also take longer to see a return on your investment. However, a full-time venture will have a greater potential for growth that can be sustained long term. Keep this in mind when starting your new venture. It will play a big part in how you plan and prepare.

3. What are you good at – Again, having a passion for the business you start will greatly improve your chances of being successful. Understanding what your strengths are will also help you achieve success. It sounds simple, but you would be surprised how many people start businesses they know nothing about. Not to say you can't be successful trying something new, but it is much easier if you have some experience. It also helps if the business aligns with your personality. For example, if you are an introvert, it may be a challenge to start a business that's rooted in sales. Likewise, if you are an extrovert, you may find it hard to sit at a computer all day. That said, I recommend you conduct a self-assessment. Identify your strengths and weaknesses and try you best to craft your business around them.

4. How much money do you have to risk – This one is simple. You must decide the amount of money you have to invest in your new business. Some businesses especially online can be started with little to no money. Others can take hundreds of thousands to start. Either way, decide how much you are going to start with. Once you have an amount, start researching what business match your budget. Remember, it not only costs to start a business, but it also costs to maintain it. Create a budget for at least the first year of business and set aside a contingency fund for any unexpected costs.

5. Do you want to provide a service or a product – Deciding whether to sell a product, provide a service, or both will be an important decision when creating a business. Creating a product-based business may require more upfront costs and the success of the business will weigh heavily on the quality of the product. On the other hand, service-based businesses rely more on expertise and relationships and may have a lower cost for entry. That said, product-based businesses can help to make you money while you sleep, while service-based business may require active involvement. Keep this in mind when deciding the type of business to start

5 STEPS TO STARTING YOUR OWN BUSINESS

1. Create a business plan – A goal without a plan is just a wish. When it comes to business, poor planning can be the difference between success and failure. Now when some think about creating a business plan, it can sound like a long tedious process. However, a business plan does not need to be 100 pages. In fact, I would recommend starting with a Lean Business Plan. A Lean Business Plan is a one-page outline of your business. It should address what your business will do and how your business will make money. You should also identify your target market, potential customers, and any current competitors. Next, you will want to list any key business expenses and provide a rough estimate of revenue. Lastly, try to establish at least 3 goals or milestones for your business. For example, set a 3-month, 6-month, and 12-month business goal. Once you have a draft of your lean plan, make sure you save it and review it weekly. The goal is to constantly add and adjust your lean plan as your business grows.

2. Choose a name – There is power in a name. That said, one of the best ways to spark interest in your business is with its name. Not only that, your company name is often the first thing your customers will see. In today's age of social media, your business name may be as important as the product or service you are selling. The right name will elevate your business, however the wrong one can hurt it. For this reason, you should always think long-term when creating a name for your business. Try to avoid location specific names or names that could be offensive. You want the name to be able to grow with your business. That's because your name will carry your businesses' reputation and be its calling card. Do your best to create an authentic, memorable, and web-friendly name that represents your business's image and mission.

3. Register your business – Registering your business will make it legal and protect your brand. You can create a corporation, LLC or other business entity by filing with your state's business agency. You will need to complete some basic information and pay a filing fee. Once you complete the registration, the state will send you a certificate that you can use to apply for a Tax ID and open a bank account. During this time, I would also consider buying a website address. Having a web domain and website will add credibility to your business and provide your brand with marketability.

4. Apply for a Tax ID – Once you have registered your business, you'll want to apply for an employer identification number (EIN). EINs are distributed by the IRS. An EIN is basically a social security number for your business. You will need it to obtain a business bank account. You will also need it to apply for a business credit card, obtain a business loan, and file taxes. The process is free and if you complete the application online you can get your EIN immediately.

5. Open a bank account – In the beginning, opening a business bank account is not a requirement. However, as your business begins to grow it will become increasingly more important. With that said, I would recommend doing it from the start. Having a separate account will help you organize your finances. Using your personal account for business transactions can make it difficult to account for your business spending vs your personal. Having a separate account will allow you to easily track your business expenses, payments, and receipts. Opening a business account will also add a level of credibility. In fact, it can even help build credit history for your business. All you need is an ID, EIN number, and your business registration information.

CHAPTER NINE: STARTING A NONPROFIT

With the advent of social media, there has been an increased awareness and desire to serve those in need. As you would expect there has also been an exponential growth in the nonprofit sector. Nonprofit organizations are entities created with the goal of providing public or social benefit. That could include advancing financial education, promoting music and arts, or sponsoring sports programs in underserved neighborhoods. Whatever the cause, a nonprofit is the perfect vehicle for servicing the needs of a community or even the world. Not only that a nonprofit can help to boost the credibility, goodwill, and exposure, of your business.

That is why you often see companies create nonprofits to work in conjunction with their core business. If you are thinking about starting a nonprofit, there are several things you should consider first. Below is a list of five things to consider before starting your nonprofit. Use them as a guide as you begin on your nonprofit journey.

5 THINGS TO CONSIDER BEFORE STARTING A NONPROFIT

1. Why do you want to start a Nonprofit – Just like starting a business, it is important to ask yourself why you want to start a nonprofit. Remember a nonprofit's purpose is to provide a service or benefit to the community. So, if you are looking to start a nonprofit, make sure it is for the right reason. Starting a nonprofit is not easy and they call it "nonprofit" for a reason. Most nonprofits rely heavily on volunteer work and donations. That said, I would recommend you focus on something you are passionate about and enjoy doing. Think about what motivates and inspires you. Having passion for your cause will greatly improve your chances of creating a successful nonprofit.

2. What is your mission – Again social media

has helped to bring several important causes to the forefront of the public eye. However, that has also increased competition in the nonprofit sector. That said, it will be vital for you to define your cause and the mission of your nonprofit. Your mission statement should be 1 to 2 sentences that clearly defines what your nonprofit does and who it serves. Even though it should only be 1 to 2 sentences it is a good idea to spend time on your mission statement. It will ultimately play a big part in how you plan, prepare, and organize your nonprofit.

3. What are you good at – Again, having a passion for the nonprofit you start will greatly improve your chances of being successful. Understanding your strengths will also help you achieve success. It is much easier if your experience aligns with your mission statement. For example, if you are an accountant, starting an afterschool program that teaches financial literacy would make since. Likewise, if you are a nurse, running a wellness program would also align with your experience. That said, it is always helpful to conduct a self-assessment. Identify your strengths and weaknesses and try your best to craft your nonprofit around them.

4. How will you fund your nonprofit – Nonprofit does not mean "no expense". It will take money to run your nonprofit. It will be important to know what it will cost to fulfill your mission statement. Again, nonprofits rely heavily on volunteer work and donations. Some nonprofits can be started with little to no money. Others can take hundreds of thousands to start. Either way decide how much you are going to start with. Once you have an amount, start looking into fundraising options. There are many ways to fundraise. Some of them include charity events, emails, social media, GoFundMe, and in-person. Nonprofits can also obtain local, state, and federal grants. Create a budget for at least the first year and set aside a contingency fund for any unexpected costs.

5. How will you raise awareness – Just like a business, nonprofits require marketing. This will be your main way to raise awareness about your cause and to increase donations. Again, social media is a great way to raise awareness. However, when it comes to nonprofits it is always good to add a personal touch. I would recommend reaching out to schools and churches in your community. If your nonprofit can benefit them, work to gain their support. You would be surprised how much support you can receive when you focus on your community.

5 STEPS TO STARTING A NONPROFIT

1. Conduct a needs assessment – They say give people what they need not what they want. That said, a successful nonprofit will fill that need. A needs assessment is necessary to help you identify what that need is. Think of it as an extension of your mission statement. Your needs assessment will outline what your nonprofit does, who it serves, and identify current competitors. Understanding what organizations exist in your community is somewhat more important with a nonprofit than it would be in business. That is because if there is another organization that is fulfilling your target mission, it could potentially affect your ability to fundraise. In most cases donor dollars are limited. For that reason, if you discover another nonprofit focused on your mission, consider tweaking your mission statement to address a need they are not.

2. Choose a name – Just like a business, there

is power in a name. The name of your nonprofit can elevate your organization. It should be align with your mission statement and embody the values of the organization. Remember your name will carry your businesses' reputation and be its calling card. Do your best to create an authentic, memorable, and web-friendly name that represents your business's image and mission.

3. File Articles of Incorporation –You can create a corporation by filing with your state's business agency. You will need to select a board of directors, complete the required forms, and pay a filing fee. Once you complete the registration, the state will send you a certificate that you can use to apply for a Tax ID and file for tax-exempt status. During this time, I would also consider buying a website address. Having a web domain and website will add credibility to your nonprofit and provide your brand with marketability.

4. Apply for a Tax ID – Once you have registered your nonprofit, you'll want to apply for an employer identification number (EIN). EINs are distributed by the IRS. An EIN is basically a social security number for your nonprofit. You will need it to obtain a bank account. You will also need it to apply for a credit card, obtain a loan, and file for tax-exempt status. The process is free and if you complete the application online you can get your EIN immediately.

5. File for tax-exempt status – Unlike a business, nonprofits are tax exempt. However, to establish tax exempt status you must file with the IRS. There is a fee that ranges between $275 and $600, depending on your application method. The application process can take between 3-12 months and can be found at irs.gov.

CHAPTER TEN: TAXES

Albert Einstein once said, "The hardest thing in the world to understand is the income tax". If you have ever read through the tax code, you would probably agree. Simply put tax rules can be complicated. However, depending on your tax bracket, filing your taxes could be very simple. It really depends on how much money you make. In the United States we have what is called a progressive tax system. That means the higher the income the higher the tax rate. There are currently seven federal income tax brackets: 10%, 12%, 22%, 24%, 32%, 35% and 37%. Now that does not mean the more money you make the more tax you pay. We have all heard the stories of millionaires and billionaires who pay very little or nothing in taxes. That is because in the U.S. we also have something called tax deductions. Tax deductions are subtracted from your earned income to determine your taxable income. Taxable income is the amount of a person's income that can be taxed. For example, say you earned $100,000 for the tax year and were eligible for $30,000 in tax deductions. You would only pay taxes on your taxable income of $70,000 ($100,000 - $30,000). Now this is a very simplified example. Again, the tax code is very complex and is made up of thousands of rules and regulations. For this reason, I recommend consulting a professional for complex tax scenarios. Believe me, the last thing you want is an issue with the IRS. That said, below are some basic tax tips I recommend using when dealing with taxes. Following these simple tax tips can make filing taxes a little easier each year. Remember tax planning and having a tax strategy will become increasingly important as your income rises. Do your best to stay ahead of the game when it comes to taxes. In the long run it will only save you time and money.

5 TAX TIPS

1. Follow the rules – "You have to learn the rules of the game. And then you have to play better than anyone else". This is another quote from Albert Einstein that perfectly explains how to approach tax planning and tax strategy. Remember, the tax code is made up of thousands of rules and regulations. That said, it is legally our responsibility to follow them. That means if you don't know the rules, don't play the game. I can't count the number of people that have fallen victim to the IRS due to tax issues. Whether it was due to a lack of information or done explicitly to break the rules, it is never a good idea to play around with Uncle Sam. The penalties can be harsh, and you could even end up being charged criminally. So, know the rules before you file that return. That extra credit or deduction may seem like a lot now, but could wind up costing even more in the future.

2. Keep good records – Keeping your records

organized and accessible is one of the best things you can do to avoid tax issues. The IRS recommends keeping records for 3 years from the date you file or 2 years from the date you paid the tax. This should include W2s, 1099s, or any interest income statements. You will also want to keep any records related to any deductions or credits you may have claimed. If you have a business, good record keeping is especially important. IRS data has shown self-employed people who earn $100,000 or more face audit four times more than the average taxpayer. That said, do your best to separate your business activities form your personal. I would also recommend using an app or program to track your business expenses. In the end, keeping good records will save you time and could also save you money.

3. File on time – This should go without saying but filing your tax return on time is an important rule to live by. This is especially important if you owe money. Failing to file on time when you owe money, could cost you a penalty of 5% per month. Being self-employed could cost you even more for filing late. For example, if you're self-employed and fail to file a tax return for a period of three years, you'll stop receiving Social Security credits toward your retirement. That said, you can see how important it is to at least file your return. Even if you don't have the money to pay your tax bill, I would recommend filing. It is better to file and try to work out a payment plan then not filing at all. Even though you could incur fees or penalties, it will be much less than the penalty you'd face by failing to file in the first place.

4. File an extension – If you can't file your taxes on time, the best option is to get an extension. An extension can be filed online and can give you an extra six months to get your tax return filed. There is also no cost to file extension. If you are due a return, there really is no downside to getting an extension. However, if you owe money, you will still be charged penalties and interest on the unpaid amount. That said, if you don't file, you could be charged a late filing fee on top of penalties and interest.

5. Get professional help –Taxes are complicated. If you are not confident you can handle filing your return, hire a tax professional. A good tax preparer can be well worth the fee. Especially if they can identify expenses to write off or credits you can receive. It is not uncommon for taxpayers to overpay because they did not file for or collect eligible credits. That is why the best way to guarantee nothing is overlooked and you are able to optimize your tax return is to hire an experienced and highly rated tax preparer. That said, be cautious of anyone promising to eliminate your tax debt. In most cases this just a way for them to charge you service fees. Before working with these type of tax services, try contacting the IRS yourself. In most cases you will have the same chance to negotiate a reduction as they would.

PART III: BONUS

In the final part of the book, we address family and money. We also give you 100 Life Tools & Cash Rules.

FAMILY & FRIENDS

They say love will bring a family together, but money can tear it apart. Whether its loaning money to family, financial infidelity, or doing business with friends, people will not always agree when it comes to financial matters. That's why you should use caution when mixing business with pleasure. Or for that matter, family and money. Arguments over money often ruin relationships. Have you ever seen a family member pull up in a brand-new car. The car they bought with the money they owe someone else. That said, there's no guarantee a loan will be repaid and that it won't cause conflict and disappointment. It's really how you handle the situation that will make all the difference. Money is an emotional subject, so communication is key. Don't make it a thing that no one talks about. Below you will find five tips for dealing with Family & Money. Use these tips to help you avoid any potential conflicts and resolve any issues.

5 TIPS FOR DEALING WITH FAMILY & MONEY

1. Just say no – As easy as this sounds, saying no is actually one of the hardest things to do. Many people feel obligated to help family and friends. In fact, these same family and friends may have helped them in the past. This makes saying no even more difficult. The bottom line is you must decide how important it is for that person to repay you. If they didn't repay you, would it ruin your relationship or hurt you financially? If the answer is yes, then it may be best to say no. Again, it may be difficult to say no. And saying no could still end up hurting your relationship. That said, it's not always what you say but how you say it. Make sure you listen to the request and don't say no too quickly. You can also ask for more time to think it over. However, don't take too long to respond and when you do be firm about it. That means don't say maybe or be vague. Say no and don't make any excuses or try to give an explanation. You can simply Say, "I'm sorry, but I can't give you a loan." If the person asks, "Why?" just repeat your statement.

2. Have an agreement – If you decide that you are going to lend money or do business with a family or friend, it's a good idea to put something in writing. Again, this can be a touchy subject, but it's really best for everyone. It does not have to be a long-drawn-out contract. It can be as simple as an email. Make sure to layout the terms of the agreement. If it's a loan, be sure to include the amount to be repaid and the date or timeline for repayment. If you get push back for asking for an agreement, don't do it. Someone saying, "don't you trust me?" should be an immediate red flag.

3. Give it as a gift – If the relationship is important to you and you are doubtful you will be repaid, think of the loan as a gift. A gift does not have to be paid back. If they do pay you back, then that's just a bonus. This will save you the stress of worrying about being repaid. No one wants to be the person nagging someone about the money they are owed. You can also consider giving less than the loan amount. For example, maybe they ask you for a $500 loan. Instead of loaning them $500, maybe you can just give them $100. In most cases, the person will be happy you tried to help.

4. Communicate – If a relative or friend has borrowed money from you but hasn't repaid you, address the issue as soon as possible. Decide quickly whether you're going to seek repayment or consider the loan a gift. Don't prolong the situation and let it turn into something that will ruin your relationship. Remember, the longer you let it sit unpaid the more you will have negative feelings about it. If you are unable to resolve the issue, let the person know how you feel and let it go.

5. Fool me once, shame on you; fool me twice, shame on me – If a relative or friend has borrowed money from you but hasn't repaid you, I wouldn't recommend loaning them money again. This will obviously affect your relationship with that person, but in the end, this may end up better for you. It reminds me of a part in the movie Bronx Tale. In the movie "C" is upset because Louie owes him $20 and keeps dodging him when he asks for repayment. "C" wants to hurt Louie but instead Sonny tells him "You don't even like him…Look at it this way: It costs you 20 dollars to get rid of him… He's out of your life for 20 dollars. You got off cheap". That said, think about it like this. That $50 loan that your family member didn't repay, could save you from lending them $1000 in the future.

LIFE TOOLS & CASH RULES

Below is a list of 100 Life Tools & Cash Rules. They are in no particular order, so if it doesn't apply let it fly.

100 LIFE TOOLS & CASH RULES

1. Check your interest rate – Interest rates will either save you money or cost you a fortune.

2. Track your net worth – Your net worth equals your assets minus your liabilities. It will be your financial scorecard.

3. Set a budget – A budget is the starting point for every financial goal in life.

4. Start saving ASAP – Not next month. Not when you get a raise or your taxes back. Today. Time is money and compound interest is the eighth wonder of the world.

5. Start with small debts then conquer the big ones –Paying off little debts gives you confidence to tackle the larger ones.

6. Consider an all-cash diet – Put that card away.

If you can't be disciplined, use all cash.

7. Make savings part of your monthly budget – Do not save what is left after spending. Spend what is left after saving.

8. Take a daily Money Minute – Take 60 seconds to check your accounts and track goal progress.

9. Allocate at least 20% of your income toward financial priorities – This means emergency savings, paying off debt, and long-term investments.

10. Be prepared to walk away – Don't feel obligated or pressured to make a deal. It is better to walk away than make a deal you will regret later.

11. Keep your savings account at a different bank than your checking account – Accounts at the same bank make it too easy to transfer money. Separate your checking and savings.

12. Spend on experiences not things – A flight or cruise is better than clothes or shoes.

13. Direct deposit– Start saving automatically.

You'll be surprised how much your account grows.

14. Avoid credit checks –A hard credit pull can negatively affect your credit score. Resist requests to run your credit and only do a credit application when you are sure you want to buy.

15. Shop solo – Avoid the friend that says, "You have to get it!". Shop alone.

16. Never cosign a loan –Friend, family member, significant other, or whoever don't do it. If a payment is missed your credit score is hit.

17. Get a secured credit card – A secured card can build credit like a regular card, but it won't let you overspend, and you don't need good credit.

18. Know your financing – Get pre-qualified before shopping for anything that will require credit.

19. There are 5 types of financial emergencies – Using emergency savings is only if you've lost your job, have a medical emergency, car breaks down, emergency home repair, or you need to travel to a funeral. Otherwise, just say no. Dubai doesn't count.

20. Never give up – Miracles happen every day. Put in the effort and have patience.

21. Do not cash out your retirement account – Cashing out a retirement account is only ok if you have no savings, you've lost your job, or have a medical emergency. Even then think twice.

22. Keep Your credit utilization rate below 30% – Calculate your credit utilization rate by taking the sum of all your balances divided by the sum of your cards' credit limits.

23. Give people a second chance, but not a third – Everybody makes mistakes. People deserve a second chance. However, the third mistake is not an accident its deliberate.

24. Keep your savings out of your checking account – Get separate accounts. Using your checking account as a savings account won't work.

25. Choose your spouse/mate carefully - This

decision will account for 90 percent of your happiness or 90 percent of your misery.

26. Never be the smartest in the room –If you are the smartest in the room, find a different room.

27. If you want to go to college fill out the FAFSA – Even if you don't think that you'll get financial aid, it doesn't hurt to fill out the form.

28. Never stop learning– Regardless how "successful" you've become, learning never stops.

29. Wear the same thing every day. – I wear sweat suits and tennis shoes almost every day. It is one less thing to worry about in life.

30. You can have too much savings –If you have more than twelve months' savings in your emergency account, start thinking about investing.

31. Consider joining a credit union – Credit unions can have better loans, and better interest rates.

32. Say less – Everything you say will be used against you. Don't start talking just to talk. It is ok to say, "I don't know" and even better to listen and learn.

33. Always choose federal student loans over private loans – Federal loans have flexible terms, better interest rates, and potential to be forgiven.

34. Give money to get money – Take advantage of employer matching. But you'll only get it if you contribute first.

35. You're better off being happy than being rich – Sometimes money is a prize for people who didn't get what they really wanted.

36. Travel – Travel while you're young, travel while you're old. Just make sure you travel. Get to know and respect the other cultures in the world.

37. Be open about your mistakes – Sounding too perfect is a mistake. Talk about mistakes you've made and keep it real.

38. Don't be your own worst enemy – Be your own greatest supporter. Nobody can hurt you as much as you.

39. Have a mentor and become a mentor – Learning from and teaching others is the best way to build powerful relationships in both directions.

40. Get renters insurance – It covers robberies, vandalism, and natural disasters. It could also cover damages you cause at someone else's home and rent if you have to stay somewhere else.

41. Control your emotions – The goal in negotiations and debate is to always control your emotions. Be patient and stay focused.

42. If you're struggling with student loans call the lender – Call your lender and ask if they offer graduated, extended, or income-based plans.

43. When you get a raise, raise your savings – Every time you get an increase in pay, the first thing you should do is up your savings and increase your long-term investments.

44. Your mortgage should be under 30% of your monthly income – When you're trying to figure out how much you can afford 30% is a good rule of thumb.

45. Get your finances and body in shape - More exercise leads to higher pay. The habits and discipline associated with fitness are also associated with managing your money.

46. Evaluate purchases by cost per use – When deciding if an item is worth it, factor in how many times you'll use it.

47. Avoid the extras – Learn to work with the basics. Most of the time the extras aren't worth it and only increase the cost.

48. Check your credit report and score regularly – Check your credit score monthly and set up alerts for any updates or changes to your report.

49. Get more life insurance – The basic policy from your employer is often too little. Extra life insurance will save your family.

50. Ask for what you want – People are afraid to say what they want. That's why they don't get what they want.

51. To befriend successful people, don't ask for favors. – If you want to make friends with successful people, don't ask for anything. If your successful, befriend people who don't need anything from you.

52. Eliminate toxic money thoughts –Never say "I'm broke" or "money is the root of evil". You're setting your mind up to fail. Stay positive.

53. It's okay to ask for help– Ask for help when you need it. People love to help. Don't be insecure.

54. Create a "not-to-do" list – Just because you can do anything, doesn't mean you should do everything.

55. Do less– Do fewer things. The majority of things taking up your time are distractions and won't make you successful.

56. Done is better than perfect – Continuous improvement is better than delayed perfection. Get it done.

57. Live your worst-case scenario – Hope for the

best but plan for the worse.

58. Learn how to savor – Appreciate what you have now instead of trying to find happiness by acquiring more things.

59. Study the habits of successful people – Imitation is the best form of flattery. Why try to reinvent the wheel.

60. Get a money buddy – Friends can pick up good habits from each other. Find friends who like to invest, save, and pay down debt.

61. Pay attention to fees – In the long run a bunch of small fees will be the same as a big loss.

62. Spend on the real you not the imaginary you – Don't buy for the person you want to be. Buy for who you are. If you don't know who that is, ask your bank account.

63. Confidence breeds success– Successful people have very strong egos and their supposed to.

64. When negotiating a salary, let them go first

– Your current pay could be lowballing or highballing a potential employer. Let them name the figure first and then push them higher.

65. Working for money won't make you wealthy – Making your money work for you will make you wealthy.

66. Having money is not the same as having status – You must earn respect, not buy it.

67. Budget 30% of your income for lifestyle spending – This includes anything that doesn't fall under basic necessities.

68. Draft a vision board – A vision board will remind you of your financial goals. Use it for motivation and to stay on track.

69. Adopt a spending mantra – Create a phrase that acts like a rule of thumb for spending. For example, "Is this [fill in purchase here] better than flying to Greece next year?".

70. Ditch the overdraft protection – Why would

you want to overspend, and then get charged a fee for it.

71. Invest in yourself – If you're not worth it, who is?

72. Social media is antisocial – Take a break from it and go talk to someone in person.

73. Set specific goals – Use exact numbers and specific dates. Describe what you want to accomplish in detail and full color.

74. You can negotiate more than your salary – Work hours, official title, telework, vacation time, and which projects you work on can all be negotiated.

75. Don't allow the phone to interrupt important moments – Put the phone down. It's your child's birthday party. Instagram can wait.

76. Sweat the small stuff – Enjoy the little things because one day you may look back and realize they were the big things.

77. 80 percent of success is based on your

ability to deal with people – The world involves dealing with people in some way or another. You must be good at dealing with people. If you're not, you will not succeed.

78. Choose your friends wisely – Sometimes the people you'd take a bullet for are the ones behind the trigger.

79. Not everyone will like you – That's just the way of the world. You probably won't like everyone either.

80. True wealth is everything you can't see – Your friend with the expensive car and the designer clothes could be drowning in debt.

81. Don't assume you don't qualify for unemployment – Only half the people eligible for unemployment apply for it.

82. Love yourself – People say they love money, they love traveling, and they love shopping. Ever wonder if they love they self?

83. Become the most positive and enthusiastic person you know – Being positive attracts success and successful people.

84. Don't compare yourself with anyone else – Take only inspiration from others. Remember everyone is on their own path.

85. Don't burn bridges – You'll be surprised how many times you have to cross the same river. Do you really want to spend time re-building bridges?

86. Make small money goals – The farther away a goal is, the more likely you will give up. Set short-term goals for a quick win.

87. Review your portfolio once a year – Look at your long-term investment account at least once every year. Make sure your investments still match your goals.

88. Make salary discussions about your company's needs – Your employer doesn't care why you want more money. Always emphasize the value you bring to the company.

89. Debt isn't worth it – Buying things you can't afford will give you a short-term buzz, but will leave a long-term hangover.

90. Never deprive someone of hope – Never tell people their dreams are impossible. Hope is a beautiful thing, and it could be all they have.

91. Age is perspective – When you're twenty, you think fifty is old. When you're fifty, you feel thirty. When you're seventy, fifty looks like twenty.

92. Change is good– "A thug changes, love changes, and best friends become strangers". Don't resist change.

93. Have a firm handshake – A firm handshake is necessary for making an impression on everyone you meet.

94. Keep it simple– Keep it simple.

95. Be a good winner – Be humble in victory, congratulate the losers on their effort.

96. Life is not fair – Don't expect life to be fair.

Expect it to be hard. That way if its easy, you can push right through.

97. Get comfortable with the uncomfortable – It is a form of self-discipline and a character trait needed in life.

98. Relax – Try not to worry about situations that dont have an effect on your life.

99. Look people in the eye – Looking people in the eye establishes a connection. It shows you're serious.

100. Show respect for people who work for a living – 9 to 5 or 5 to 9. They deserve respect.

ACKNOWLEDGEMENT

Thanks to everyone who encouraged and inspired me to write this book.

ABOUT THE AUTHOR

Jay Robinson

Jay "CPA" Robinson was born in the great state of Michigan. He grew up as an only child and was raised by his mother. As a child Jay had aspirations of playing professional basketball. He grew up idolizing the Fab Five and continues to be a fan of the University of Michigan. Unfortunately, after being kicked off of his H.S. basketball team, his dreams of being in the NBA began to diminish. However, he did manage to play a year of college basketball at Morris Brown College in Atlanta, Georgia. After spending a year in "Hotlanta" he returned home with a new perspective on life and a newfound passion for entrepreneurship. It did not take long before Jay quickly realized he had outgrown his hometown. It also didn't take long for his mother to see it was time for a change, and she secretly sent off his application to attend Howard University. He says one day he came home, and his mother says "Start packing. You're moving to D.C.". Jay would spend the next four years in "Chocolate City" and eventually would graduate from the Howard University School of Business with a major in accounting. As a young man, Jay never imagined he would grow up to be an Accountant. However, a conversation with his Uncle convinced him that if he wanted to be in business, accounting was the best path. That said, twenty years later, Jay has enjoyed a successful career in accounting.

Along the way he has also dabbled in entertainment, real estate, finance, and now writing. Jay currently resides in Prince George's County Maryland just outside of Washington, DC. Jay is married and has 3 children. In his free time, he enjoys traveling internationally and lists Santorini, Hurghada, and Dubai as some of his favorite destinations. Jay also enjoys working on DIY projects and hanging out by the pool. One of his favorite quotes comes from Malcolm X "The future belongs to those who prepare for it today".

www.ingramcontent.com/pod-product-compliance
Lightning Source LLC
Chambersburg PA
CBHW071356210526
45465CB00001B/121